UNIFIED ACTION HANDBOOK SERIES

This *Handbook for Military Support to Economic Stabilization* is Book Four in a set of five handbooks developed to assist the joint force commander design, plan, and execute a whole-of-government approach. Included with the series is an overview J7/J9 Pamphlet, *Executive Summary of the Unified Action Handbook Series*, that describes the handbooks, suggests how they should be used, and identifies the significant interrelationships among them. The following is a short summary of each handbook:

Book One: *Military Participation in the Interagency Management System for Reconstruction and Stabilization*

The handbook outlines joint force roles and responsibilities in the Interagency Management System (IMS) and existing interagency coordination authorities and mechanisms. It aligns with the *USG Planning Framework for Reconstruction, Stabilization, and Conflict Transformation*. It will also align with the *IMS Guide* under development at the Department of States' Office of the Coordinator for Reconstruction and Stabilization.

Book Two: *Military Support to Essential Services and Critical Infrastructure*

This handbook defines services essential to sustain human life during stability operations (water, sanitation, transportation, medical, etc.), the infrastructure needed to deliver such services, and potential joint force responsibilities.

Book Three: *Military Support to Governance, Elections, and Media*

The last comprehensive guide to military governance was written in 1943. Combatant commanders have directed joint forces to rebuild media, support election preparations, and provide advisors to embryonic executive ministries and legislative committees in recent and current operations. This handbook provides pre-doctrinal guidance for joint force support to good governance, political competition, and support to media.

Book Four: *Military Support to Economic Stabilization*

This handbook outlines joint force support to economic development. It addresses conducting a comprehensive economic assessment, employment and business generation, trade, agriculture, financial sector development and regulation, and legal transformation.

Book Five: *Military Support to Rule of Law and Security Sector Reform*

This handbook defines the "Rule of Law;" explains the interrelationship between rule of law, governance, and security; and provides a template to analyze the rule of law foundation essential to successful stability operations.

NOTICE TO USERS

All approved and current Joint Warfighting Center (JWFC) Pamphlets, Handbooks, and White Papers are posted on the Joint Doctrine, Education, and Training Electronic Information System (JDEIS) Web page at https://jdeis.js.mil/jdeis/jel/template.jsp?title=jwfcpam&filename =jwfc_pam.htm. If a JWFC product is not posted there; it is either in development or rescinded.

PREFACE

1. Scope

This *Handbook for Military Support to Economic Stabilization* provides established and evolving techniques and procedures used by joint force commanders (JFCs) and their staffs in planning, executing, and assessing joint force support to economic stabilization during post-conflict conditions.

2. Purpose

This handbook's primary purpose is to provide the JFC and staff with a common, practical baseline of "best practices" and inform doctrine writers, educators, and trainers about joint force support to civilian-led economic stabilization. It also may serve as a bridge between current practices in the field and their migration into doctrine.

3. Background and Content

a. Over the past several decades, the Department of Defense (DOD) has learned many lessons while conducting stability operations in Bosnia, Kosovo, Somalia, Afghanistan, Iraq, and elsewhere. Although FM 3-07, *Stability Operations*, provides a basic foundation for military activities across all five stability operations sectors, there has been little doctrine or guidance published specifically for military support to economic stabilization. Consequently, this handbook is intended to provide more detailed guidance at the operational level on the range of functions required to achieve stability in post-conflict situations and to help identify specific economic stabilization-related tasks that may be required of joint forces to support stability operations. It presents commonly used definitions and constructs from the interagency and international communities that have been harmonized with joint doctrine, and discusses those "best practices" that have proven valuable during on-going joint operations, exercises, and experimentation. It stresses the importance of coordination with external organizations, defining supported and supporting roles, and focuses on considering economic factors during planning.

b. While the handbook defines and discusses many potential military roles related to economic stabilization, there is no implication that US forces will automatically undertake any or all of these in a given instance. Rather, the handbook lays out the range of options available to support the process of economic stabilization, and special factors that may need to be taken into account. The information in this handbook also can inform recommendations to higher-level authorities regarding possible economic stabilization activities.

c. As the United States Joint Forces Command continues to interact with the combatant commands, Services, and civilian agencies; we recognize that there is no universal methodology on how military support to economic stabilization is planned and conducted, nor should there be. Because of this realization, this handbook is a documented approach to ensure that commonly accepted, effective, and proven "best practices" are identified and integrated into joint force operations and doctrine.

4. Development

a. JP 1-02, *Department of Defense Dictionary of Military and Associated Terms*, defines unified action as, "The synchronization, coordination, and/or integration of the activities of governmental and nongovernmental entities with military operations to achieve unity of effort." To this end, United States Joint Forces Command (USJFCOM) embarked on a multi-year "Unified Action" project to carry forward the principles of unified action through concept development and experimentation. This project focused on two lines of operations (LOOs) to achieve its objectives. The first line included limited objective experiments contributing to the implementation of the DOD work plan to support National Security Presidential Directive 44 (NSPD-44). The second LOO included spiral events to produce a series of handbooks and overview (see inside of the front cover). The products of both LOOs were developed and validated through a rigorous process of experimentation that was conducted with military and civilian partners across the United States Government.

b. This handbook was developed in close coordination with, and used significant input from, both civilian and military subject matter experts. The authors also regularly vetted the content with these experts to assure currency and accuracy of both theory and practice. The guidance and TTP in this handbook also are based on existing joint doctrine, best practices refined during current operations, and observations from exercises, experimentation, and prototyping. As a result, it represent the current state of best practices regarding economic stabilization.

c. An important issue which arose during the drafting of this handbook is the widespread use of jargon and acronyms that may not translate particularly well between various agencies within the US Government (USG). Insofar as possible, the authors have attempted to improve the readability of this handbook by using common terms in plain English. This handbook also includes a glossary of terms commonly used within the interagency community that may not be familiar to military planners.

5. Application

While this handbook does contain extracts from some doctrinal publications, it is not approved joint doctrine, but is a non-authoritative supplement to currently limited doctrine that can assist commanders and their staffs in planning, executing, and assessing economic stabilization-related activities in concert with civilian authorities and agencies. **Commanders should consider the potential benefits and risks of using this information in actual operations**. Further, commanders may want to tailor specific elements to conform to their individual staff requirements, operations, and operational environment.

6. Distribution and Contact Information

a. Distribution of this handbook to USG agencies and their contractors is authorized. Other requests for this document shall be submitted to USJFCOM, Joint Concept Development and Experimentation, Attn: Maj Arnold Baldoza, 115 Lake View Parkway, Suffolk, VA 23435-2697; or by phone to Maj Arnold Baldoza at 757-203-3698.

b. Comments and suggestions on this important topic are welcomed. The USJFCOM JWFC points of contact are Lt Col Jeffrey Martin, 757-203-6871, jeffrey.martin@ jfcom mil; and Mr. Dave Spangler, 757-203-6028, david.spangler.ctr@jfcom mil.

DAN W. DAVENPORT
Rear Admiral, U.S. Navy
Director, Joint Concept Development
& Experimentation, J9

STEPHEN R. LAYFIELD
Major General, U.S. Army
Director, J7/Joint Warfighting Center

Intentionally Blank

TABLE OF CONTENTS

APPENDIX

GLOSSARY

FIGURE

TABLE

CHAPTER I
ESTABLISHING PRIORITIES

"We know that at least in the early phases of any conflict, contingency or natural disaster, the U.S. military – as has been the case throughout our history – will be responsible for security, reconstruction, and providing basic sustenance and public services. I make it a point to reinforce this message before military audiences, to ensure that the lessons learned and re-learned in recent years are not forgotten ...."

Secretary of Defense Robert M. Gates

THE MILITARY PROBLEM

What economic factors should be considered during the Joint Operational Planning Process, what resources are available, and what other organizations should be engaged during design and planning?

---

1. Overview

a. For the joint force, supporting economic stabilization represents enabling the economic conditions that usher in the nascent stages of growth allowing for the resumption of commercial activities. These conditions include re-opening and operating businesses, the increase of or the reversal of downward trends in private sector employment, and re-establishing or maintaining functioning markets. It does not necessarily mean returning to the status quo, or conditions that existed prior to a conflict, particularly if they were the drivers of the conflict.

b. Whenever military forces conduct stability operations, they generally focus initially on securing and safeguarding the populace, reestablishing civil law and order, and restoring public services and key infrastructure. Indigenous, foreign, or US civilian subject matter experts (SMEs), rather than US military personnel, typically perform many of the non-security stability operations tasks. However, because of the frequently hostile post-conflict environment, the military's dominating presence, the ability to control forces, local logistics capabilities, or the lack of such capacities by other agencies, US military forces are directed by Department of Defense (DOD) policy to be prepared (preferably for a short period) to lead the activities necessary to accomplish these tasks. Once legitimate civil authority is prepared to conduct such tasks, US military forces will transition to a supporting role.

2. Early Engagement

a. Because the DOD must be prepared to conduct stability operations throughout the range of joint operations, planning for likely post-conflict requirements related to the economy should begin as early as possible. As noted by the US Agency for International Development (USAID)[1], early attention to the fundamentals of economic growth increases the likelihood of successful prevention of a return to conflict and movement forward to renewed growth. To ensure proper focus, joint planning must reflect the right balance between the economic, political, security, and humanitarian requirements in the operational environment. Striking that balance, which will be unique to the country and phase of the intervention, may require acceptance and reconciliation of incompatibilities between these requirements. Although stability operations are normally short-term, planning should consider the impacts on longer-term economic programs and initiating long-term programs as soon as the opportunity exists. While the pace of economic stabilization will depend on basic security and essential services restoration, it is imperative to move quickly at an early stage to re-engage in economic development broadly:

"Paul Collier, an Oxford University economist and leading expert on African economies, argues that external peacekeepers and robust economic growth have proven to be more critical than political reform in preventing a return to conflict. Accordingly, many interventions geared to facilitate economic growth can and should be implemented at the very beginning of the rebuilding process, much earlier than traditionally has been the case." (USAID), A Guide to Economic Growth in Post-Conflict Countries (2009).

The USAID Guide goes on to stress:

"Early emphasis on providing humanitarian assistance and expanding physical security must be accompanied by programs to provide jobs and critical public services, and reconstruct key economic infrastructure."

b. USAID uses the illustration in Figure I-1 below[2] to illustrate the relative level of effort required in the various economic growth program areas over time. While requirements will vary depending on the conflict, security and humanitarian assistance may account for over 50% of the initial effort, which emphasizes the relative importance of security to economic stabilization.

c. In the aftermath of a conflict or crisis, the US military will likely have a broad array of partners, many of whom will have expertise in specific areas that the military lacks. Many of these organizations participated in handbook development in order to achieve consistency in the methodology used to assess situations, identify opportunities, develop programs, and prioritize resource allocation across the spectrum of interventions. Identification of organizations with specific expertise provides the reader a good start point to facilitate coordination. The military's role should be to provide security first to "stop the bleeding" in the short-term; and prepare to transition responsibility to appropriate civilian agencies for the long term.

3. Context

a. Because of the complexity of the economic system following a conflict, each chapter includes a discussion on how to assess the economic situation, placing particular emphasis on the likely social and political impact of economic recovery activities. The first chapter of the handbook gives an overview of a process that can help quickly identify and prioritize critical problems related to the economy, using readily available information. Subsequent chapters review how planners may design and evaluate courses

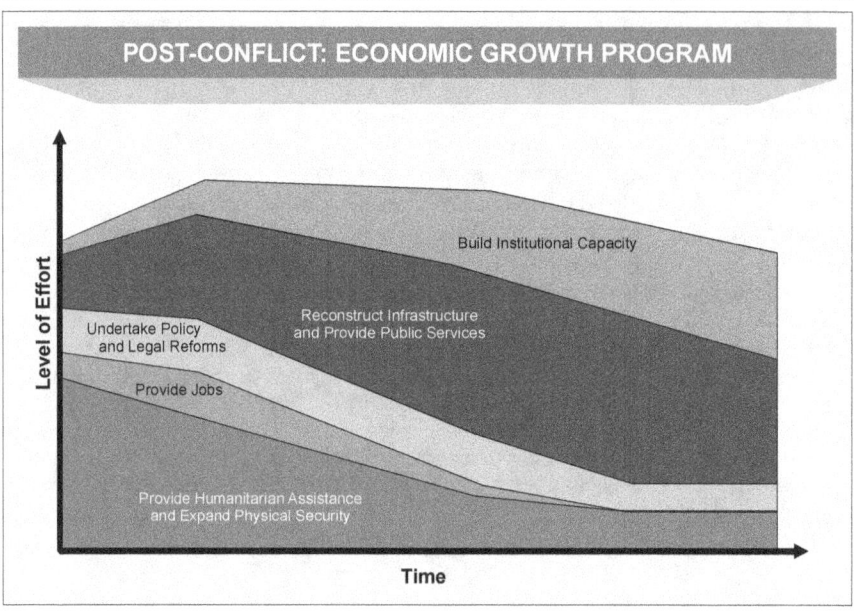

Figure I-1. Post-Conflict Economic Growth Program

of action to address specific problems in key sub-sectors of the economy. These sub-sectors include generating employment, restoring commerce and the private sector, reviving trade and investment, linking producers and consumers to markets, encouraging agriculture, and supporting monetary stability and the expansion of financial services. Each chapter provides guidance concerning metrics, and includes vignettes and case studies of past stability operation efforts highlighting a number of "best practices".

b. Although this handbook focuses on military support to economic stabilization, planning should integrate economic considerations with respect to security, governance, infrastructure, and other sectoral considerations, to accomplish the mission better. For example, if the focus is solely on employment generation for economic stability, without regard to social reconciliation or the principal of nondiscrimination, joint force actions may actually cause more instability. Planning should also include undertaking immediate tasks to restore normal economic activity with a view toward transitioning these to more mid- and longer-term efforts. There is no magic switch that, when flipped, will result in a healthy economy; rather, a series of combined and integrated actions should be used that result in positive complementary effects over time.

4. Coordination

a. The long-term goal of economic stabilization is to contribute to societal stability, support efforts to restructure security forces, disarm, demobilize, reintegrate combatants, and reconcile segments of the population. Historically, achieving stability generally requires an extended period and the coordinated efforts of domestic and international partners, most of which are civilian agencies, or reside in the private sector. Accordingly, Joint Force Commanders (JFCs) should plan to establish and participate in and use mechanisms to coordinate with the HN government, international organizations, and nongovernmental organizations (NGOs) with regional expertise and experience in nation building. Coordination with various host-nation and civilian actors will be labor-intensive, and will generally be at least as important as the essential tasks themselves. In this context, Joint Force efforts should focus on security, and initiate reconstruction and stabilization efforts that build upon more immediate humanitarian assistance and disaster relief (HA/DR) requirements and activities, and set conditions for follow-on civilian efforts. The goal is to start the area in question on a path to societal stability, market-based economic growth, job creation, and an invigorated private sector. As noted above, it is important to move on a broad range of fronts early, at a phase when that country is most receptive to accepting fundamental change. In doing so, it is especially important that efforts be informed by policy, and supportive of other related efforts.

b. **Functional Specialists**

(1) Combatant command or JTF planning staffs may be provided functional specialists with stability operations competencies through the civil affairs planning teams (CAPTs) from the appropriate regionally aligned civil affairs command within the US Army Reserve or from individual augmentee reservists provided by the Services. These competencies may include individuals whose functional area specialty relates to economic stability. They can be a resource to coordinate with interagency and international organizations focused on the economic sector. However, current demands for meeting rotational requirements has caused the services to focus on training and sustaining a generalist civil affairs force with less emphasis being placed on the need for providing qualified functional specialists.[3] In the event functional specialists are absent, this handbook provides planners a place to start the process of coordination with organizations in the economic sector until specialist become available to assist in planning.

(2) It is often important to make sure the staff has access to even more focused levels of expertise, as required. For example, the staff may need experts in economic planning, assessment, collection, economic data interpretation, skills to coordinate directly with USG agencies, expertise in employment generation, agriculture, and finance. If the JFC does not have or cannot obtain the required expertise to reside with the staff, planning must include a robust capability to reach back to access assistance from relevant USG agencies through established legal mechanisms.

c. There are some terminology differences between DOD, the interagency, and international organizations of particular note. DOD uses the term "assessment" to mean "a continuous process that measures the overall effectiveness of employing joint force capabilities during joint operations," or the "determination of the progress toward accomplishing a task, creating an effect, or achieving an objective."[4] However, the interagency and international community uses the term "monitoring" in a similar way to mean "the collection of routine data that measure progress toward achieving program objectives."[5] They use the term "evaluation" to mean the use of measures to determine "how well the program activities have met expected objectives and/or the extent to which changes in outcomes can be attributed to the program or intervention."[6] Therefore, when we are trying to get typical DOD "assessment" data we need to be asking for monitoring and evaluation (M&E) data. The interagency and international communities use the term "assessment" to mean the up-front collection of information to determine the current state of the environment and situation.

    d. Contracting versus Command Lines of Authority. Figure I-2 illustrates the difference between command and contracting lines of authority. Contracting authority differs from command authority. Contracting authority does not follow the same line of authority as command authority (to include operational control and tactical control), but does follow a similar path of administrative control. Contingency Contracting Officers (CCOs) receive their contracting warrants from a source of contracting authority, not command authority. During contingency operations, contracting organizations within the Joint operations area (JOA) will be staffed with senior contracting officials (SCO) through whom all contracting authority will flow. There will be at least one chief of contracting office (COCO) reporting to each SCO. The COCOs are forward deployed to

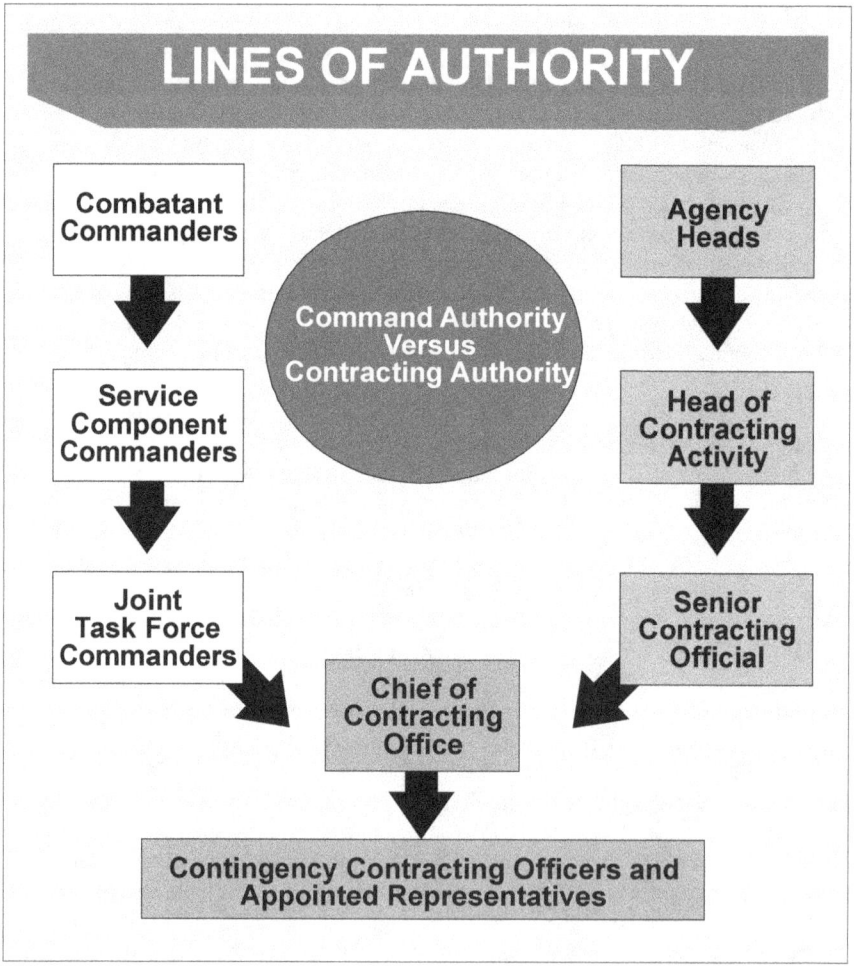

Figure I-2. Lines of Authority

the theater of operation and are staffed with CCOs and CCO appointed representatives who provide contracting support to their customers.

e. **Command Authority**. Combatant command (command authority) includes the authority to perform functions involving organizing and employing commands and forces, assigning tasks and designating objectives, and giving authoritative direction over all aspects of an operation. It does not include authority to make binding contracts or obligate funds on behalf of the United States (US) government. Commanders at all levels must avoid improper command influence, or its appearance, on the contracting process. The contracting officer must be able to independently exercise sound, unbiased business judgment and contract oversight in the accomplishment of the contracting mission.

f. CCO-appointed representatives may fulfill their role as part of an additional duty assignment or even from a different geographic location than the CCO. For this reason, the representative must maintain near constant communication with the CCO. The representative's primary duty must not present or create a conflict of interest with their additional duty as a representative. As with a contracting officer, the unique personal responsibilities of a CCO-appointed representative means supervisors, commanders, and others who have administrative control over them in their role as a representative must avoid directing them to take actions that might violate laws or contracting regulations. The relationship between a CCO-appointed representative and their operational command can be especially complex. In their primary duty, outside of being a CCO-appointed representative, they are subject to traditional command authority. In their additional duty as CCO-appointed representative, they are subject to contract authority. Prior to selecting an individual to become a CCO-appointed representative, both the command and the individual must understand and delineate the duties and responsibilities under both authorities and consider the affect it may have on the performance of the representative's primary duty.[7]

5. International Economic Stabilization Principles

Joint planners need to understand the underlying economic stabilization principles that govern other USG and international development agencies in order to better coordinate and synchronize activities. The following are basic principles for promoting economic stabilization in post-conflict settings, based in part on the Organization for Economic Cooperation and Development (OECD) *Principles for Good International Engagement in Fragile States*,[8] USAID *Nine Principles for Reconstruction and Development*, and others:

a. **Take country context as the starting point**.[9] It is important to understand the policy, strategy, environment, and performance of a country's economy. The constraints of a HN government's capability, capacity, political will, legitimacy, and physical environment are important considerations when planning stability operations. Participating in a collective assessment and working as part of a whole of US Government (USG) (or whole of coalition) strategic response is the best way to achieve this understanding.

b. **Focus on institutional capacity and state-building as the central objective.** Good governance and economic stabilization go hand-in-hand; and a focus on institutional capacity and state building makes short-term efforts easier to relate and transition to the longer-term strategic program. This is not institutional reform, which is difficult and takes a long time. It is important to emphasize the importance of host nation ownership and building the country's capacity to administer its institutions legitimately. Establish the following modest goals:

(1) Ensure security and justice. Security is the military's greatest contribution and is the principal prerequisite for stability across all sectors. It is particularly important in economic stabilization.

(2) Mobilize revenue, providing basic services, and generating employment. After providing physical security to the host population, assuring basic sustenance is the second most urgent task. Economic stabilization only has meaning in a society after survival is reasonably expected.

c. **Plan, organize, and measure progress toward achieving objectives that address the drivers of conflict and institutional capacity**. While joint doctrine provides several recommendations for constructing logical lines of operation (LOO) in an operation, most examples have used either the national instruments for the projection of power (diplomatic, informational, military, or economic (DIME)), or functions (maintain security, develop governance, and facilitate civil administration). Planning and organizing around objectives can facilitate greater coordination among functions, because objectives often cut across many of the functions. This requires different functions to come together and be involved in LOO development and execution. Examples of this might be to plan and organize around lines of operation like "counter external support to insurgency" or "ensure the country's oil reaches international markets." The latter LOO example would clearly involve security, economic stabilization, infrastructure development, civil administration, governance, and other functions. This is consistent with State Department's *Principles of Planning Framework for Reconstruction, Stabilization and Conflict Transformation,* which states that "Major Mission Elements (MME) therefore must be a narrow tailored set of outcome [objective] statements that are together necessary and sufficient to achieve the overall policy goal [end state] within the stated timeframe. Stating MME as objectives will help planners avoid stove-piped responses based on current capabilities." Each LOO typically affects multiple systems that act as receptors of influence within the operational environment: political, military, economic, social, informational, and infrastructure (PMESII). Each function and system within a LOO requires full-time assessment, coordination with other stakeholders, and involvement of all relevant staff sections from across the joint task force (JTF) and the AMEMB. These objectives focus on diminishing drivers of conflict and increasing HN institutional capacity to deal with them. When HN institutional capacity exceeds the drivers of conflict, some would say that we have achieved sustainable peace.[10]

d. **Use existing processes and coordination mechanisms to partner with appropriate organizations**. The Office of the Secretary of Defense (OSD) and the Joint Staff (JS) coordinate with other federal departments and agencies, and those of coalition and other partners, using various mechanisms. The country team, under the Chief of Mission, is the existing and proven coordinating mechanism in the field. This existing and proven field coordination mechanism holds true for joint force conduct of activities that support economic stabilization. The joint force should avoid supporting or conducting economic stabilization activities in isolation and must understand the US country team's strategy for economic stabilization, including any economic agreements or arrangements the AMEMB country team may be implementing with the HN. Joint Publication (JP) 3-33, *Joint Task Force Headquarters*, flexibly defines military structures to handle complex challenges requiring coordination of all elements of national power. Additional joint and Service doctrine and directives should also be referenced and used, for example, JP 3-57, *Civil-Military Operations*, JP 3-07.3, *Peace Operations*, and JP 3-08, *Interagency, Intergovernmental Organization, and Nongovernmental Organization Coordination During Joint Operations*.

6. Coordination Processes

a. **Interagency**. OSD and the Joint Staff will lead military participation in whole of USG assessment and planning, and the JFC will coordinate through and with them. The coordination process is either using the Interagency Management System,[11] co-led by the National Security Council (NSC), State Regional Assistant Secretary, and Coordinator for Reconstruction and Stabilization (S/CRS) if activated, or the National Security Council Interagency Policy Committees. The primary contributors to the economic stabilization assessment are USAID and Departments of State and Treasury. The Departments of Homeland Security, MCC, Commerce, Agriculture, Health and Human Services (HHS), Energy, Labor, and others may also participate as appropriate.

(1) **Department of State**

(a) The Secretary of State coordinates and leads integrated United States Government (USG) efforts, involving all US departments and agencies with relevant capabilities, to prepare, plan, and conduct reconstruction and stabilization activities. When directed by the Secretary of State, S/CRS will coordinate interagency assessment and planning for integrated USG reconstruction and stabilization efforts. Activation of the Interagency Management System (IMS) enables an Interagency Policy Committee (IPC) or the Country Reconstruction and Stabilization Group (CRSG) to accomplish this. If not, the Chief of Mission and State Department Regional Assistant Secretary or Bureau of Political Military Affairs will lead interagency assessment and planning.

(b) **The American Embassy (AMEMB) country team** and its economic section is one of the most important sources of reliable information and analysis. In addition to a State Department economic officer, many embassies have an USAID mission responsible for managing US development assistance programs. Many embassies also have a Department of Commerce Foreign Commercial Service office staffed with personnel who are familiar with commercial conditions and with US trade and investment; and some embassies have an agricultural affairs section staffed by the Department of Agriculture personnel. A complete listing of AMEMB contacts for economic, commercial, agricultural, and USAID assistance programs in each country is under "key officers" on the State Department website.[12]

(2) **US Agency for International Development**. USAID advances US foreign policy objectives by supporting economic growth, agriculture and trade, global health and

democracy, conflict prevention and humanitarian assistance. USAID has Foreign Service Officers (FSO) posted in US Embassies throughout the world and, as described previously, prepare country assessments. The USAID mission will also be able to provide an overview of foreign and international assistance programs. The USAID Office of Military Affairs also has liaison officers at each GCC who serve as development advisors. In the immediate post-conflict/crisis, USAID Office of US Foreign Disaster Assistance (OFDA) deploys Disaster Assistance Response Teams (DART) that provide immediate "on the ground" assessment, and work routinely with other aid organizations. At the strategic level, coordination with USAID is through OSD and the JS using the IMS, or more routine NSC processes. At the operational and tactical level, coordination is through the GCC liaison and Office of Defense Cooperation or Military Groups in the country team.

(3) **Department of Treasury**. Regional offices in the Under Secretary of Treasury for International Affairs coordinate Country Economic Assessments with other Department of Treasury offices (principally the Under Secretary for Terrorism and Financial Intelligence and the Office of Technical Assistance). The Secretary of Treasury also represents and serves as the US Governor on the boards of the IMF, World Bank, Asian Development Bank, African Development Bank, European Bank for Reconstruction and Development, and Inter-American Development Bank. The Department of Treasury coordinates policy and information sharing with these and other financial institutions.

(4) **Department of Commerce**. The Department of Commerce has an Office of Reconstruction and Stabilization that can coordinate extensive capabilities throughout the various Agencies and Bureaus. In addition to the Foreign Commercial Service global network of trade professionals, it has regional bureaus and offices that possess detailed knowledge of local conditions and actors.

(5) **Department of Agriculture (USDA)**. Two offices contribute directly to assessment. The Economic Research Service (ERS) is USDA's principal social science research agency. ERS conducts agricultural and economic research, market analysis, and produces socioeconomic indicators. The Foreign Agriculture Service (FAS) is responsible for collecting, analyzing, and disseminating information about global supply and demand, trade trends, and market opportunities. FAS seeks improved market access for US products; administers export financing and market development programs; provides export services; carries out food aid and market-related technical assistance programs; and provides links to world resources and international organizations. The FAS supports the USDA contribution to the S/CRS Civilian Response Corps and represents USDA in interagency country assessments.

(6) **Department of Energy**. The Regional Offices (under the Assistant Secretary for Policy and International Affairs), the Assistant Secretary for Electricity Delivery and Energy Reliability, and the Energy Information Agency all conduct assessments in their respective areas and can contribute to an overall interagency country assessment.

(7) **Departments of Homeland Security, Transportation, Labor, Health and Human Services; US Trade Representative; Overseas Private Investment Corporation; Export-Import Bank; US Trade and Development Agency; and Millennium Challenge Corporation**. Each of these departments and agencies brings specialized expertise and

each has many bureaus and agencies that can contribute useful knowledge to an assessment. The agencies are best engaged through the JS, OSD and S/CRS using the ICAF or the IMS and NSC processes.

b. **International**. A number of international organizations maintain large databases related to global, regional, and country-level (to include sub-national) economies as well as publish topical analysis. Joint forces should coordinate through the JS and OSD using existing mechanisms to access these important sources of information. The most important of these are:

(1) **IMF and World Bank**. Both the World Bank and the IMF have instruments to assist countries as they emerge from conflict. They normally lead initial assessments, coordinate short-term priorities with the host nation, and help meet substantial needs for technical assistance by formulating plans for delivering technical assistance into the medium term. The World Bank in conjunction with other donors also finances medium- and long-term structural adjustment programs in the education, health, infrastructure, communications, and other sub-sectors aimed at improving the competitiveness of a host country economy. The IMF publishes data (available through its website[13]) on its lending to countries, international exchange rates, other economic and financial indicators, and maintains the *World Economic Outlook* database. The World Bank publishes data, research, and analysis related to development, including the *World Development Indicators* database of over 800 indicators related to development and the *Doing Business* data series detailing business conditions. Both databases are accessible though the World Bank's website.[14] Data on individual country conditions and programs are also available on the World Bank web site.

(2) **The United Nations (UN) Office for the Coordination of Humanitarian Affairs** (UNOCHA) mission is to mobilize and coordinate effective and principled humanitarian action in partnership with national and international actors. It operates through a network of field offices, which support UN Humanitarian Coordinators and country teams. It also maintains regional support offices and Regional Disaster Response Advisors in Africa, the Caribbean and Latin America, the Middle East, and Asia Pacific. Joint forces should engage through existing mechanisms, primarily through the USAID OFDA. The UN maintains the *Relief Web* site,[15] which is an on-line gateway to documents and maps on humanitarian emergencies and disasters. As an independent source of information, designed specifically to assist the international humanitarian community in effective delivery of emergency assistance, it provides relevant information as events unfold.

(3) **The UN Development Program** (UNDP) is a specialized UN agency designed to promote human development. The UNDP maintains a database with statistics on a wide range of development indicators related to literacy and education, health, employment levels, economic output, energy production, poverty, labor rights, CO_2 emissions, and conventional arms transfers. The UNDP database is accessible through the UNDP website.[16]

(4) **The UN World Food Program (WFP) and Food and Agriculture Organization (FAO)** are the UN frontline agencies in the fight against hunger. Both

organizations respond to emergencies, assess needs and devise programs that help transition from relief to reconstruction and development. These organizations may be active in countries where other agencies may not be able to operate and can provide information on conditions. Joint forces should request this information through the AMEMB country team, State Department Humanitarian Information Unit, or USAID.

(5) **The World Trade Organization** (WTO) deals with the rules that govern international trade at a global or near-global level. The WTO maintains a database with tariff and trade profiles of over 180 countries, and statistics on international trade in merchandise and commercial services. The database is accessible through the WTO website.[17]

(6) **The International Civil Aviation Organization** (ICAO), a specialized UN agency, maintains a database on airports, economic regulation of aviation, and agreements that govern global civil aviation. The databases are accessible through the ICAO website.[18]

(7) **Regional Organizations**. Additional information on economic and financial conditions and government and regional programs to stabilize economies, promote growth, and reduce unemployment may be available from regional organizations. Examples include the Asian Development Bank, InterAmerican Development Bank, and the Association of Southeast Asian Nations (ASEAN).

(8) **Allies and Regional Business Partners**. Information on business and economic conditions may also be available from the governments of countries allied with the United States, particularly if they are located in the same region, have historical ties or their companies have stronger commercial ties. The OECD Development Cooperation Directorate Development Assistance Committee website[19] lists most major countries and links to country websites. Regional trade partners may also be an important source of information.

(9) **Host Nation (HN) Partners**. Similar to the US Department of Commerce, most countries have organizations that are responsible for collecting and analyzing economic data. Frequently, the central bank and/or Ministry of the Interior will collect monetary and other economic data. After conflict, the mechanisms that these organizations use to collect data may not be reliable due to lack of funding, disintegration of means to collection data, and lack of trained personnel. Supporting or establishing this capability may be an important post-conflict task.

(10) **Business organizations at the local, regional or national level** can often provide information and insight on the economy.

(a) Organizational considerations may include geographic location (similar to a chamber of commerce) or line of business (like US trade associations). Labor organizations or unions, if present, may be a source of information on employment conditions. The US country team and the Department of Commerce (International Trade Agency) are most knowledgeable of the appropriate organizations.

(b) Key business leaders can often provide valuable sources of information related to the operation of military-sponsored programs, such as efforts to generate employment or remove security-related and other impediments to the flow of commerce in local areas. They may also offer anecdotal information and insight into the political dimensions of the economy as well as into business conditions and specific problems. The US country team facilitates engagement of these leaders.

(11) **Nongovernmental Organizations** (NGOs). Many large NGOs release material online relevant to economic reconstruction and can be located through the internet. Of particular relevance is the Center for International Private Enterprise (CIPE), a nonprofit affiliate of the US Chamber of Commerce, which provides management assistance, practical experience, and financial support to local business organizations to strengthen their capacity to implement democratic and economic reforms. The Joint force should use USAID and the Department of Commerce, through the JS and OSD, to interface with NGOs and trade associations for operational level planning. The Joint force should use the country team for collaboration and planning with these organizations while in the HN.

c. **Multinational**. When part of an international military coalition, all of the coordination described above with interagency and international organizations needs to occur. Coalition operations, however, adds another layer of required coordination, because each nation has to coordinate with their own interagency and habitual processes while working toward unified action across the force. The benefit is that the capability that the coalition can access should be much greater than any nation on its own. Coalition coordination efforts should include synchronization of all economic stabilization-related support programs, funds, and activities as well as commander's discretionary funds with other interagency and international efforts across the area of responsibility (AOR) to optimize creation of the desired effects. Coalition planning should also provide efficiencies in dealing with regional or international organizations/process, facilitating a comprehensive approach. Finally, integrating public affairs and information considerations into all operations to support a coherent communications strategy can provide a beneficial synchronization of words, images and actions and optimize positive outcomes.

7. Developing an Economic Stabilization Situational Awareness

a. Post-conflict economic stabilization and rebuilding involves planning and executing activities to help a country emerging from conflict reduce the risk of returning to conflict, provide for the well-being of its population, and promote political and social stability. This will require a good degree of situational awareness on the part of the JFC and his staff. FM 3-07, Stability Operations, states that economic assessments are critical to the success of economic recovery programs. JFCs and staffs must understand the economic conditions in the operational area, the factors that affect stabilization and growth, and the cultural nuances that influence how the market sub-sector performs. Developing a shared understanding of the economic situation spurs market integration, helps to identify key needs and opportunities, increases private sector participation, and improves social and economic cohesion throughout the host nation. Including economic stabilization considerations during the Joint Operational Planning Process (JOPP) requires an assessment of the pre-conflict and likely post-conflict state of an economy to provide an understanding of the economy dynamics and interactions with the other PMESII systems. This understanding is crucial to mission analysis and developing potential courses of action. Appendix A provides a recommended approach to conducting a comprehensive rapid assessment using readily available information, and meaningful engagement with other USG departments and agencies. *Principles of Interagency Conflict Assessment Framework* (ICAF) is a USG approved approach to enabling an interagency team to assess conflict situations systematically and collaboratively; and it supports USG interagency planning for conflict prevention, mitigation, and stabilization. This collaboration provides a shared awareness of USG strategic objectives, and informs the identification, prioritization, and sequencing of prospective military tasks supporting economic stabilization and rebuilding. In some cases, there will be little need for the joint force to conduct comprehensive end-to-end assessments, because relevant data will be available from other sources (e.g., USAID, Economist Intelligence Unit (EIU), UNDP, and World Bank). However, in conflict prone areas, data may be missing, incomplete, old, inaccurate, or only based on assessments conducted in certain sub-sectors and geographic regions (like the capitol), which may not deliver a complete picture to a planner. Therefore, it is important to review external data for currency, accuracy, and completeness before incorporating it into the assessment plan, effort, or decision-making process.

b. An assessment of anticipated post-conflict economic conditions for purposes of military planning is fundamentally different from a post-conflict assessment conducted by civilian agencies and organizations. While civilian agencies may have a wider range of experience in post-conflict reconstruction and stabilization, they are not normally prepared to operate independent of joint support in a hostile,[20] or uncertain[21] security environment, or where control by a national government has effectively ceased. In contrast, military forces must be prepared to begin stabilization operations in hostile and uncertain environments with many of the most fundamental economic stabilization tasks directly related to, and dependent upon, security. These may include reestablishing a secure environment in which individuals can freely go about their daily business enabling commerce, protecting records relating to ownership of property and other assets, protecting or restoring critical infrastructure, and protecting government assets from destruction and looting. Because security will affect much of the effort to stabilize an economy in the immediate post-conflict period, the assessment should identify those tasks for which:

(1) Primary responsibility for immediate implementation rests with the military. These may be heavily security-related tasks.

(2) Civilian agencies retain responsibility, but which military forces need to be prepared to execute, especially when security conditions do not permit large-scale civilian deployment. The range of tasks is potentially broad, and may include employment generation to restore essential services and emergency infrastructure, support to banking institutions, fiscal and budgetary assistance and technical help to restore basic ministry functions. These requirements emerge rapidly in the aftermath of cessation of hostilities. The US Institute of Peace has highlighted the importance of the period toward or right after the end of conflict, by designating it the "golden hour." As described by James Stephenson, "One term used in emergency medicine is the golden hour. The military learned in Vietnam that if a wounded soldier received medical treatment at a field hospital within one hour, he would probably survive. In post-conflict transition terminology, the golden hour refers to the first year after the end of hostilities. Unless the population senses steadily improving conditions in that first year, popular support for change and

whoever is in charge declines, and the chances for economic, political, and social transformation begin to evaporate, enabling recidivism and even insurgencies."[22] The first few weeks of an intervention's golden hour is the time when the intervention force creates a new power structure and environment. It is easiest to establish new institutional practices during this period. Typically, governance deficiencies are primary causal factors of the crisis, therefore improving these systems as soon as is practical to correct them.

        (3) Civilian agencies will execute missions that may require some level of joint support. These tasks are most frequently associated with humanitarian assistance, but can include other activities related to security sector reform (SSR).

    c. Coordinating an assessment of economic activity within stability operations should be integrated into the overall assessment effort and begin, if possible, before operations have commenced. While reliable data and information may be limited, some questions concerning the post-conflict environment may require estimation during an assessment, and assumptions made in mission analysis. Examples are the physical condition of economic infrastructure, availability of credit and banking services, established bartering systems, food supply and access, status of basic health services, and knowledge about how the informal market is operating, among other things that enable an economy to function. As directed in DOD Instruction (DODI) 3000.05, Stability Operations, joint plans, and especially the assumptions, should be integrated, exercised, and gamed with other US departments and agencies. It is important to understand the economic environment, the conflict impact, and current requirements in order to properly prioritize and sequence activities for military forces to undertake at the appropriate moment. In many conflict prone countries robust bartering systems have been established; considerations must be taken into account as to the effect the influx of cash will have on this type of informal economy. Be prepared to initiate or support civilian capacity building efforts when the security environment allows. The lessons of recent interventions have demonstrated that successful, sustainable post-conflict reconstruction is dependent on establishing security, the rule of law, good governance, and creating conditions conducive to private economic activity, the sequencing of which must be driven by local conditions and context.

CHAPTER II
EMPLOYMENT GENERATION

"Job creation projects are one of the most effective means for stabilizing communities and keeping the peace immediately after conflict, offering a fundamental basis for healing and reconciliation. Employment provides access to resources, generates confidence in the future, creates a stake in an expected recovery and moderates the conditions of want that may have been the root causes of the conflict."[23]

Kenneth W. Beasely 2006

The Military Problem

What are the military's leading and supporting roles in immediately generating job opportunities? What resources are available, what other organizations should be engaged in the planning, and what organizations should assume responsibility for projects?

---

1. What is the Issue?

Generating employment is both an immediate peacekeeping and post-conflict objective, and a means of establishing the foundation for future economic growth and political stability. The primary emphasis in the immediate post-conflict period is to provide employment quickly, even if those jobs are temporary and not sustainable. If joint forces can pay young men to pick up shovels, it is a better alternative to picking up guns to work for the enemy. Even though the military focus will be on quickly implementing short-term efforts, it is essential that the military and civilian agencies have a common understanding of the problems and risks, and work to align short-term efforts to support civilian agency longer term economic and political development strategies. Coordinated planning should consider political and social dynamics, host nation institutions, private sector development, and requirements for a viable peace. The UN High Commissioner for Refugees (UNHCR), who has championed quick acting programs, states "Unless Quick Impact Programs form part of an integrated strategy for reintegration, rehabilitation and reconstruction, and designed with community participation their impact is likely to be insufficient, isolated and short-lived."[24] Ideally, joint force projects should provide immediate and visible impact to the local population, support the legitimacy of the host nation government, create linkages to other efforts, and stimulate follow-on activity.

2. Why is Employment Generation Important?

Effective employment generation programs in the immediate post-conflict environment assist in restoring economic activity, addressing economic, humanitarian, and social needs, particularly in areas where lack of security and inoperable infrastructure restrict private enterprise. Employment opportunities can also support achievement of the political objectives by encouraging dislocated populations to return to their homes, providing benefits to former combatants, and giving potential "spoilers" viable alternatives to warfare and banditry. Key determinants of the nature of the military role in employment generation will be the general security environment, the condition of the economic related infrastructure, the scope of the need for employment generation programs, and the access of civilian responders to the area.

3. Operational Relevance, Objectives, and Effects

a. Design of economic stabilization objectives include prevention of a return to conflict, instilling a sense of hope and optimism toward the future, and minimizing potential conflicts with medium and long-term development objectives.

b. In order to achieve these objectives, joint force support for creation of the following effects/conditions may be helpful:

(1) A safe and secure environment exists that facilitates economic activity necessary to generate employment.

(2) Transportation and other physical infrastructure required to support commerce are available (thereby enabling employment generation).

(3) Spoilers do not benefit from economic stabilization projects.

(4) The percentage of key population groups engaged in productive economic activity increases.

(5) Participation in all levels of the education system increases.

(6) Unemployment in key population groups decreases, while overall employment in sustainable activities increases.

(7) Average wage levels increase and are sustained locally without the need for USG or donor sponsored programs.

4. General Planning Considerations

"To provide security you need to engage people. You need to tackle unemployment. You need to create job opportunities, substantial opportunity so people would be more involved in their well being rather than explosives and insurgency."

Ayad Allawi, Prime Minister of Iraq (2004-2005)

a. **Understand the status** of existing or planned USG, regional and international programs that support employment generation. The AMEMB country team can provide this information while helping to ensure that any planning initiative is consistent with the AMEMB's Mission Strategic Plan and Country Assistance Strategy.

b. **Involve USG agencies**; plan for a Tactical Conflict Assessment; and determine the necessity for military-sponsored employment programs. Assess the need before planning major military-sponsored job creation programs, because establishing a secure environment by itself may promote employment and economic activity. In countries where USAID operated a field mission pre-conflict, consult closely with it and other USG agencies and NGOs with experience in community-based programs that allow residents to participate in the rebuilding process. Plan to conduct a Tactical Conflict Assessment that will involve local community leaders, and can highlight previously successful job creation efforts. These may have been performed by local HN government, NGOs, or national-level HN economic development organizations, and may offer valuable resources for planning guidance and potential project implementers. Determining appropriate joint supporting roles that enable resumption of these activities should be a primary focus.

c. **Create security conditions needed to facilitate employment creation**. Assist with providing security for all employment activities, not just US-financed projects, as conditions and resources permit. Determine the major sources of employment, ongoing programs, and the conflict impact. Consider the physical locations, infrastructure, political, and social issues associated with initiating both short-term employment generation activities and planning for broader based job creation as the economy stabilizes. Establishing an environment where the local population is able to move to and from potential employment is essential. Prioritize soliciting the views of local leaders (people of influence from both public and private sector) to identify threat perceptions and constraints to population movements.

d. **Identify and request necessary financial and human resources**. Plans should include a request for special accounts funds and programs for employment programs, similar to the CERP fund in Afghanistan and Iraq, to implement programs quickly. The USG currently lacks a flexible interagency funding source to conduct multi-faceted conflict prevention strategies that would help build the capacity of foreign partners to conduct reconstruction and stabilization operations. However, there is an initiative between the Departments of State and Defense that would align responsibility, authority, and resources to implement integrated US plans to build foreign partner capacity under the dual-key authority of the Secretaries of State and Defense. It is also important to recognize that the skills needed to organize, manage and evaluate job creation projects may not be available within the military or local population. For more information on the purpose and use of special accounts funds and programs like CERP, see the DOD Financial Management Regulation 7000.14-R, Volume 12: Special Accounts Funds and Programs, Chapter 27: Commander's Emergency Response Program (CERP).

e. **Request experienced field personnel**. The skills to organize manage and evaluate job creation projects are unique and may not be available in the HN immediate workforce. While joint force sponsored CERP programs have been successful in short-term job creation, some have criticized their undermining longer-term efforts or creating undesired effects. Coordinating with local stakeholders and other donors through the Joint Civil-Military Operations Task Force (JCMOTF), a Civil Military Operations Center (CMOC), or similar coordination mechanism, can mitigate this risk. Likewise, using existing donor coordinating mechanisms and leveraging civilian agency (especially USAID, the Department of Labor, and others) skills and experience can help to more quickly develop and manage job creation programs. The coordination mechanisms utilized will depend upon conditions on the ground.

f. **Anticipate the Transition from Joint to Civilian Program Management** and plan actions supportive of the long-term strategy. Joint forces can provide immediate support for quick-impact job creation, but the programs often do not support long-term solutions. To maximize project effectiveness, planners should ensure project sequencing with the work of international civilian agencies and private sector efforts to ensure continuity of effort with employees, functions, and support. The military's role is to help restore normalcy and fill the gap until civilian-led, longer term programs commence. Cooperative planning with other agencies can link short-term emergency programs and transition with long-term HN and private sector employment-generating initiatives. Based on assessment work already carried out in preparation for post-conflict intervention, planners should already know the demographic and economic characteristics of the working-age population, as well as skill levels, infrastructure, availability of credit, and entrepreneurial capacity of the population. The assessment should enable planners to identify local project potential support for national-level programs and strategies. Recent experience in Iraq and Afghanistan has shown that not nesting local projects with larger strategies often results in projects in one area having an unintended negative effect in another geographic area, sometimes in seemingly unrelated areas. Communication with HN officials at all levels and USG agencies can mitigate this risk. If coordinating mechanisms do not exist, Joint forces can facilitate this by establishing a CMOC or similar mechanism.

g. **Potential Immediate Joint Sponsored Employment Projects**. Military forces can immediately generate employment opportunities for the civilian population in numerous ways. Among proven interventions:

(1) **Support Local Public Works Projects**. Establish and operate job creation programs that directly employ targeted segments of the population to further the economic and political objectives of the mission. Local organization is optimal. Examples include basic clean up and restoration efforts managed as a cash-for-work program, aimed at ex-combatants or workers who lack viable alternative employment. 'A clear understanding of how major pre-crisis employers were affected by the crisis, and what they need to resume operation, can help establish whether there is a need for a direct job creation program by the military, as well as to help set priorities in early job creation efforts. Soliciting direct input from community leaders in the development of guidelines for project lists can help identify potential issues, support local priorities, and build local sense of ownership. Achieving the latter objective helps restore community cohesion. The US Army Corps of Engineers SWEAT (Sewer, Water, Electricity, Academics, and Trash) manual offers a useful tool in assessing infrastructure needs and suggestions for short-term restoration. The UNHCR *Quick Impact Projects Provisional Guide* also provides guidance and recommendations. Some moderate planning can ensure these do not become unproductive "make work" projects, but rather short term infrastructure restoration and employment programs that complement the planning and implementation of future, longer-term, infrastructure and employment development efforts. Examples include repairing roads and utility infrastructure to support commerce activities, restoring school systems to educate and develop the workforce, restoring basic agriculture, and supporting the re-establishment of banking facilities. Focusing on projects to restore basic agriculture,

transport, and utility infrastructure that can support economic activity can pay strong dividends. However, any project that reduces the likelihood of a return to conflict by providing employment is acceptable, such as trash collection, road and bridge repairs, and rehabilitating local clinics and government buildings. The planning considerations for these projects include:

(a) Supporting efforts to facilitate any short-term project include public information, outreach, and a communication strategy that emphasizes the project's temporary nature, and eliminates expectation of sustained employment.

DAY LABOR PROGRAMS IN IRAQ

"We started day labor programs throughout the city to help clear trash and rubble, as well as provide an economic shot-in-the-arm to these devastated communities. These day-labor programs were all planned and executed by company commanders, and their effect was dramatic. We have funneled over $5 million in aid to these programs and have employed over 15,000 Iraqis. All this happened in about three months. This decentralized economic development program only used about 10 percent of my reconstruction funds, but has accounted for over 70 percent of new employment in Ramadi. These programs have cleaned neighborhoods, uncovered caches of munitions, and have restored hope and pride to the citizens of Ramadi."

**COL John W. Charlton, USA,
Commander of Camp Ar Ramadi, Iraq
Max Boot, "More News from Ramadi,"
Commentarymagazine.com, 7/17/2007**

(b) If the nature of the project is a municipal service that would normally be provided by a local government, then it should be planned with local leaders and transitioned to the local government, as soon as feasible. Trash projects should not be long term.

(c) Contracting with a local firm, vice direct employment, is the best approach. This relieves joint forces of tasks such as hiring and firing, recording hours, paying in local currency, and other administrative employment tasks. Contracts should include protections to preclude diverting funds from employees, timesheet irregularities, and phantom workers.

(2) Hire local civilians directly as support personnel, but take precautions that wages do not distort the labor market, or the demands of US-led employment programs drain the supply of skilled and semi-skilled labor from the market. In the case of the UN peacekeeping mission to East Timor, mission hiring amounted to 10-12% of employment in the formal labor market. Studies suggest that such hiring drains the available trained labor from local industry and can cause inflationary pressures because the UN can afford to pay higher wages. In Iraq, the USAID Inspector General found that wages paid for trash pick-up were higher than the average for skilled laborers[25] and there is anecdotal evidence that translators employed in Kosovo were practicing physicians. The initial post-conflict assessment should anticipate this problem.

(3) Create secure markets, and request assistance in assessing the viability of special economic zones (SEZs). Establish secure areas where civilians can engage in commerce and productive activity. This satisfies the initial requirement to start economic activity. SEZs[26] have helped develop exports and create jobs for over 30 years. SEZs have the potential to improve security, minimize the risk to infrastructure, improve property rights enforcement, and improve business access to land by easing development process through government involvement and guarantees. SEZs can act as a catalyst to rebuild the business environment, attract investors and provide secure employment venues for vulnerable groups. The World Bank Group Foreign Investment Advisory Service (FIAS) has extensive experience in Latin America and East Asia, and most recently in Africa. Planners should consider SEZs in planning cooperatively with the AMEMB country team, the regional desk officers in the Departments of State, Treasury, and USAID.

(4) Linking job seekers to employers is important. Establishing mechanisms (e.g., employment centers) that assess skill levels and local business requirements can facilitate this until government agencies or private associations can assume responsibility.

(5) Consider support to the restart of state owned enterprises (SOEs). Planners should verify USG policy on privatization and identify the potential political or social consequences linked to SOE employers when considering options to generate employment that involve existing enterprises. Did they discriminate in favor of certain population groups; or was management corrupt and too closely linked to unpopular government figures? When considering these, there will be a trade-off between the benefit of providing employment, economic losses, and unintended effects on peacekeeping and longer-term economic reforms. Revitalizing SOEs brings people back to work, assists in the restoration of basic services, and reinvigorates production of consumer goods. Reopening even a small number of SOEs shows commitment to progress and restores a sense of normalcy. However, decisions to revitalize SOEs should include a conflict assessment to evaluate the potential negative impacts on the political reconciliation process, as well as a conventional economic analysis related to efficiency, competitiveness, and the long-term sustainability. SOEs often have strong links to the government in power prior to the crisis; and the conflict assessment should reveal whether funding these enterprises increases funding for elements opposed to the reconstruction and stabilization process. Whether and to what extent to re-start or support recovery of SOEs in the short-term will involve trade-offs at times between sub-optimal choices. Decisions taken early on do not necessarily set the course for longer-term policy.

(a) The economic assessment should reveal if there is over-employment, the general physical condition of the enterprise, the financial viability and sustainability, corruption and other factors. These assessments should be whole of USG efforts. Subsequently, through a tactical conflict assessment, joint forces should develop an understanding of local actors who may be empowered because of revitalization and encourage those persons to support the peace process. As demonstrated by experience during the UN administration of Kosovo, where the focus was primarily on state-owned public utilities, the wealth-power relationship should promote peace rather than fuel violence. As noted by the US Institute for Peace[27], if not carefully executed, well meaning schemes to revitalize economic activity could inadvertently empower spoilers and fuel conflict. Planners must emplace safeguards to ensure that those empowered do not perpetuate conflict. These safeguards include real-time oversight, audits, boards of directors, and payroll mechanisms designed to benefit employees and limit corruption.

        (b) Even existing private sector enterprises may pose challenges in cases where these entities benefit from close government ties or corruption. JFCs and military planners need to understand that "corruption" is a relative term and means different things in different social contexts. Applying a strict western zero-tolerance standard for corruption may be unworkable, and may lead to an overall net deficit in post-conflict recovery. However abhorrent it may seem, corruption is ingrained in some societies as a privilege of status and is seen as a legitimate cost of doing business. JFCs and planners have to assess, in concert with interagency representatives and the country team, how much corruption is "too much" for the post-conflict stabilization and recovery enterprise. However, USG funds that support economic stabilization programs are still governed by USG laws that outline the rules for the purpose and specific uses of the fund. Despite the HN cultural view towards corruption, these US laws must be followed and represent a limit for JFCs and planners when supporting economic stabilization efforts.

        h. **Develop a Communication Strategy**. Because public perceptions, confidence, and other effects in the cognitive dimension directly affect economic stabilization activities, it is imperative that the joint force develop a communication strategy and integrate it into the planning process. The strategy should integrate all communication capability, such as public affairs, information operations, and defense support to public diplomacy. Likewise, the communication strategy should leverage all communications means and methods that are effective in the local environment. To achieve an effective synchronization of words, images and actions requires communication strategy integration into all planning, execution, and assessment activities. For more information, see the JWFC *Commander's Handbook for Strategic Communication* and Communication Strategy, version 2.0, 27 October 2009, at the following link: http://www.dtic mil/doctrine/doctrine/jwfc_pam.htm.

5. Specific Planning Considerations

        a. Address the links to disarmament, demobilization, and reintegration (DDR). Either the UN or other authority will most likely initiate a DDR program as part of the peace process. Joint forces often assume support roles, especially in disarmament. The UN defines reintegration as sustainable employment and income, and considers it the hardest part of a DDR program to resource and implement.[28] Short-term joint force initiated employment projects need to be coordinated with the national or international DDR program. This is usually through USAID.

        b. Use labor-intensive techniques for short-term immediate-need reconstruction projects. Large-scale construction programs developing state-of-the-art facilities are usually not effective or advisable during in the immediate post-conflict period.[29] The length of time needed to contract, conduct consultations with the host nation, and design these types of projects extends beyond the immediate post-conflict phase. Staffing and maintenance can soon emerge as a critical constraint. Planners should give preference to small grassroots projects that use HN-appropriate technology and can be implemented immediately, properly staffed, and maintained. Labor-intensive techniques can create large-scale employment and income generation, and therefore contribute to long-term development. They can also contribute to instant stimulation of the local economy by providing access to markets and facilitating the circulation of information and other exchanges. If foreign contractors are used, they should begin immediately to hire and train local workers and subcontractors on a wide range of projects, not only to create jobs, but also to provide some evidence of progress in the rebuilding process.

      c. Include women in job creation programs. Women are often the most needy and least cared for in postwar societies. In many situations, they are the head of the household and must provide for their families. Assistance to women is essential, and they should be included in programs that will help them put food on their tables, care for their children, and restart lives disrupted by war. USAID and the Department of Labor have experience in planning for this.

      d. Entrepreneurs are critical. Entrepreneurs are a special group of leaders who see opportunity in the market place, have the skill to gain control of resources, take measured risk, and produce the good or service that is wanted in the market place. Entrepreneurs are the primary employers in countries with free markets, and find a place to operate in all economies. Success in creating sustainable employment centers on supporting entrepreneurs and promoting entrepreneurship. The first step in supporting entrepreneurs is to provide relatively safe environments for people to conduct business. The safe zone markets in Baghdad are a good example.

REBUILDING INSTITUTIONS IN IRAQ

"One of the key lessons of Iraq reconstruction was an often invalid assumption that pre-conflict Iraqi institutions were broken, primitive, or insufficient. In fact, the pre-conflict Iraqi judicial system was relatively sophisticated and independent, and only required assistance in returning to its former functionality. US efforts sometimes assumed that the system needed to be built from the ground up, when in fact what it needed was to be understood, allowed to exist unmolested, and enabled to succeed."

**LtCol Butch Bracknell, USMC,
Rule of Law Coordinator, Marine Regimental Combat Team 5, Al Anbar
Province, 2008**

      e. Protect businesses from theft and extortion, whether from criminal elements or public officials. Extortion is a disincentive for entrepreneurs to grow their business and hire more employees. Among key steps for supporting entrepreneurs is strengthening the rule of law. Any engagements that lead to effective contract enforcement, eliminate unnecessary regulation of business, and ensure clearly defined, easily transferable, and fully enforced property rights are good steps in strengthening the rule of law. Strong rule of law provides the foundation for entrepreneurs to build a strong economy that employs many people. Of course, many entrepreneurs will be in the market regardless of the laws. In conflict environments, considerable commerce takes place outside formal market structures and relationships. As local economies struggle to re-establish formal markets, there are strong incentives for these "conflict" entrepreneurs to use their skills for organized crime or as warlord entrepreneurs. The goal is for effective entrepreneurs to operate and employ workers in the legal market and not become spoilers. Building the right incentive structure is the key to accomplishing this goal. The goal is for effective entrepreneurs to operate and employ workers in the legal market and not become spoilers. Existing, mature, sophisticated pre-conflict legal systems may be sufficient to ensure legal protections for commerce to encourage entrepreneurship and economic recovery. Existing systems may simply need to be re-started, enabled, or refined, and may not require complete overhaul, revamping or reinvention. Building the right incentive structure is the key to accomplishing this goal.

f. Where possible, use local electronic payment mechanisms. In contracts or military-led programs to generate employment, the preferable method of payment is electronic banking. It ensures direct delivery of wages to employees, can help reduce fraud, and provides deposits to the bank. If a banking system is unavailable, a plan for cash disbursements that includes transport, distribution at various times and locations, and security of currency and the recipients is required. Use of food-for-work programs involve significant logistic and distribution plans, and need to be sensitive to not adversely affect market driven food distribution networks, related marketplaces, and local food prices.

g. Many different types of approaches can generate employment for specific constituencies. Refugees, IDPs, women, young men, and former soldiers each require unique approaches, may pose special challenges, and have needs that overlap. In post-conflict environments, the challenge of integrating youth into employment generation programs becomes even more complex. Military services during the conflict, or organizations engaged in the security sector, often recruit young men—and sometimes women— without any prior opportunity to learn viable job skills. This creates groups of young men and women that will frequently lack education or any job skills except firing a gun. Until the intervention meets this group's needs, the incentive remains for them to destabilize a fragile peace. The integration of training with remedial education delivers the best results. The best ways to ensure that they can be part of the rebuilding process includes bringing youth leaders into broader economic development strategies and creating youth organizations that empower young people. Because of the specialized nature of building this type of process, the joint force is unlikely to have the needed expertise. Planners should design these programs in close coordination with USAID, the Department of Labor, and other civilian donors.

h. Because many cultures love sports, rehabilitating buildings, fields, and other general support to sports programs in areas of high unemployment adeptly address social problems such as crime, drug, and alcohol abuse.

"After security and macroeconomic policies, the business enabling environment is the most important element for encouraging and sustaining growth."

USAID, "A Guide to Economic Growth in Post-Conflict Countries"

i. Sometimes doing nothing is the preferred course. In economics, it is often better to "do nothing," than to disturb the complex balance of forces that has evolved over many years. The military conflict itself may have been the result of disturbing this delicate balance of forces (and incentives). Understand the power of incentives and proceed cautiously.

6. Private Sector Development

a. World Bank research[30] shows new decisions about investment in existing or new firms usually depend on the availability of five basic factors:

(1) Political and economic stability and security

(2) Clear, unambiguous regulations

(3) Reasonable tax rates that are equitably enforced

(4) Access to finance and infrastructure

(5) Appropriately skilled workforce

b. After initiatives to provide immediate employment, especially for ex-combatants and potential spoilers, Joint force economic stabilization planning should focus on strengthening the capacity of relevant economic institutions supporting private sector development. The objective is to make operating in the lawful and peaceful economy more beneficial, moving economic activity from the "informal" market into the formal one. This effort requires building capacity not only in national ministries but also at sub-national levels to assume responsibility for government services as well as provide for a rule of law, and a predictable regulatory regime, which fosters private sector development sustainable jobs, and incomes.

c. Planning considerations for private sector development include:

(1) Evaluate HN government support to micro and small enterprise development by working with the AMEMB country team, USAID and the local HN government to remove regulatory obstacles that inhibit small business. Two good World Bank resources evaluate the private sector, identify constraints, and provide recommendations.

(a) The World Bank *Investment Climate Assessment*.[31] For individual countries, the assessment evaluates the state of the private sector, identifies key restraints to increasing firm productivity, and identifies policies that will alleviate obstacles and improve productivity. This provides an authoritative source to start a dialogue.

(b) The World Bank *Doing Business*[32] report (referred to earlier) provides objective measures of business regulations and their enforcement for 181 countries. It presents quantitative indicators on business regulations and the protection of property rights that enhance business activity and those that constrain it. The data provides a general indication of the local economy's performance, but more important, provides indicators for monitoring microeconomic activity. For each of the 181 countries, *Doing Business* provides a quantitative measure of existing regulations for starting a business, dealing with construction permits, employing workers, registering property, getting credit, protecting investors, paying taxes, trading across borders, enforcing contracts, and closing a business. *Doing Business* also tracks reforms made by countries over the prior year, providing trend analysis of progress in liberalizing markets and regulatory regimes that affect business development. Applying the *Doing Business* assessment of the crisis region can identify impediments to starting, maintaining and growing business and employment and will offer planners insights into the laws and regulations that shape daily economic activity.

(2) During dialogue with USG actors and the host government, planners should consider these most important regulatory reforms:

(a) Create one-stop shop for starting a business.

(b) Streamline project clearances for construction permits.

(c) Make working hours more flexible.

(d) Strengthen mechanisms that support legitimacy and enforcement of contracts and property rights. Understand how property claims are resolved locally and use that mechanism. If none exists, consider facilitating a locally administered, out-of-court, enforcement mechanism.

(e) Minimize interference in prices (subsidies, taxes, interest rates, etc.), especially reducing taxes in registering property

d. Assess the state of private sector financing and opportunities for microfinance. Joint forces can facilitate microfinance. Although there may be few banks willing to provide business and consumer loans in a post-conflict environment, there are many microfinance institutions willing to provide capital to small businesses, and many NGOs and websites who link investors to poor borrowers, or support potential business borrowers in making business plans and lending applications. Joint forces may become a facilitator between the population and these institutions by supporting the physical establishment of financial service technology centers. USAID should be the first source for assistance because they have extensive experience in microfinance and may provide additional planning considerations.[33] The World Bank also has extensive research on microfinance.[34]

e. Plans for growth in the formal economy that will operate parallel to substantial informal economic activity can provide initial growth. The informal economy refers to economic activity, either legal or illegal, that is neither taxed nor monitored by a government and is not included in official estimates of a country's economic output. This covers a broad spectrum, such as street vendors, cash paid day laborers, women who sew clothing for their own family's use, farmers who harvest and sell illegal crops, and persons who engage in human trafficking. In a post-conflict country most economic activity, and consequently employment, is likely to be in the informal economy. Joint forces should generally avoid interfering with any economic activity that is providing livelihoods for the population that is not supporting criminal or spoiler groups. For example, regulations that restrict the informal economy should have a clear public benefit that outweighs the possible negative impact on economic activity. A long-term goal should be to move informal activities into the formal sector by addressing the factors that discourage these activities from operating in the formal sector. A large informal economy may indicate a high level of disenfranchisement from the government. Getting an accurate measure of the level and extent of the informal economy can be time consuming and the risk of inaccurate data is high, but it is an important metric.

 f. Determine how to restore food security by promoting recovery in subsistence and small holder agriculture. Agriculture provides immediate livelihood and can stimulate off farm incomes and employment while helping local populations meet basic food requirements. Also, encourage establishment of cooperatives for producers, especially farmers. Cooperatives can provide for efficient community use, purchasing, and marketing. USAID, USDA, and the Department of Commerce can provide technical assistance in establishing cooperatives, which can also serve as a mechanism for community cooperation and reconciliation. Local organization is most effective. Close consultation with State, USAID, and USDA may enable provision of appropriate seeds, tools, fertilizer, fuel, pesticide, equipment, technical assistance and other required production capability to farmers. Previous DOD funded programs in post-conflict environments have used National Guard and Reserve personnel with farming and agricultural backgrounds to implement such programs – especially in environments deemed to be hostile or uncertain.

 g. Support entrepreneurs using public-private partnerships. Sustainable economic development does not come from foreign assistance alone; it requires domestic investment. Joint force comparative advantages in the areas of security, facilitation, logistics, and communication can encourage and facilitate the formation of partnerships between public and private institutions.

"We have joined efforts with organizations like the Iraqi/American Chamber of Commerce (IACC) to help revitalize small business in Ramadi. Company commanders went through every neighborhood and conducted assessments on all small businesses so we could help jump-start the small business grant program. We collected over 500 assessments, which helped the IACC begin its grant operations. This is the same technique we use with all non-military organizations— we use our presence in the city and access to the population to facilitate their operations. Revitalizing small businesses in Ramadi will lead to more stable communities, which helps us maintain overall security in the area."

**COL John W. Charlton, USA,
Commander of Camp Ar Ramadi, Iraq
Max Boot, "More News from Ramadi,"
Commentarymagazine.com, 7/17/2007**

h. Determine how creation of community centers can support private sector recovery. Community centers can provide the venue for skills training, business training, mentoring, access to microfinance and other business services. Establishing community centers has historically proven most effective where local economic civil society groups, business groups, chambers of commerce, and other organizations participate and exercise local ownership. USAID, the Department of Commerce, the US Trade and Development Agency, the International Chamber of Commerce and others can all provide assistance.

i. Determine how to provide security by contracting with local private vendors. Providing security for business and markets is the primary consideration, but contracting with the local private sector for goods and services can provide additional support to private sector development. Prioritize local private contractors for construction, repair, and other requirements. Joint forces should contract with local firms for support, equipment and supplies to the maximum extent possible. This helps create opportunities for local and host national entrepreneurs, and directly stimulates the local economy. The details of this are the responsibility of the Contingency Contracting Officer who can locally acquire the items needed to support the mission.[35]

CONTRACTING LOCAL FIRMS IN IRAQ

The Army Corps of Engineers' Gulf Region Division and Joint Contracting Command – Iraq made contracting with local Iraqi firms a priority. Reconstruction contracts built in incentives for prime contractors in Iraq to subcontract with local Iraqi businesses, including Iraqi women-owned businesses. In September 2006, more than 70 percent of the Army Corps of Engineers projects were directly contracted, mostly with Iraqi firms. Ultimately the Iraqi First program was implemented by Multinational Force Iraq. It operated on the premise that money already being spent on contracts for goods and services to support Coalition Forces can be directed to Iraqi businesses and labor. This directly supported the leveraging of contracting resources and activities to provide increased opportunities for the economic expansion, entrepreneurship, and skills training for the people of Iraq.

---

j. Incorporate the role that diaspora resources play in post-conflict economic recovery. Such resources may come in the form of capital, technical help, political support and the like. World Bank and USAID studies have shown that remittances from migrants alleviate poverty and help raise levels of child health, school attendance and investment. The USAID Global Development Alliance Diaspora Networks Alliance (DNA) can leverage the vast resources of Diaspora communities. It includes philanthropy, a volunteer corps, direct investment, and other engagements. The World Bank has also successfully implemented projects that recruit expatriates through a merit-based system to build capacity in government departments and agencies. As discussed under banking and finance, small informal money and foreign exchange dealers, such as "hawalas" or black market peso exchanges (not formal banks) transfer remittances from migrant workers. Joint forces should seek to avoid interfering with hawalas and other informal financial institutions and try to legitimize, rather than drive out of business, small foreign exchange dealers.

7. Key Interagency Partners and Coordination Processes

a. Multiple US and international agencies can provide funding and technical support for employment generation projects. The Department of State, and S/CRS when directed, coordinates civilian agency responses to crisis and post-crisis reconstruction and stabilization situations. The State Department will typically direct S/CRS to get involved when the scope of the reconstruction and stabilization effort will exceed the capability of the AMEMB and country team. This may trigger DOS activation of the Interagency Management System that is designed to assist Washington policymakers, Chiefs of Mission (COMs), and JFCs manage complex R&S engagements by ensuring coordination among all USG stakeholders at the strategic, operational, and tactical/field levels.[36] In areas where the international donor community is active, donor coordination groups may already exist that can facilitate coordination of donor and NGO actions. These extant institutional arrangements should be the preferred means of coordinating reconstruction activities. It is possible that, in the early post-crisis periods, the Joint Force will be required to establish ad hoc collaboration mechanisms to coordinate activities with the State Department, USAID, and other involved agencies.

b. Civilian agencies and organizations with employment generation capabilities are outlined below:

(1) The **AMEMB country team** is the principal for planning and coordination. The country team will generally have at least one economic officer, a USAID mission director and possibly officers from the Departments of Commerce, Treasury, Agriculture and others. These officials will be the best positioned to advise the joint force on the current situation as well as programs already sponsored by the host government, the USG and other donors. All these offices receive support from their respective Washington based headquarters as described below.

(2) **USAID** is the main partner for the joint force for local economic stabilization coordination. The USAID OFDA deploys a DART and works routinely with other organizations in fragile states and in post-disaster environments that are providing humanitarian assistance. The USAID Office of Transition Initiatives (OTI) works with civilians in fragile states using quick impact projects lasting 2-3 years and has extensive experience in generating employment. The USAID Conflict Mitigation and Economic Growth offices also support initiatives that support economic stabilization. All these offices operate through issuing contracts to implementing partners/NGOs and providing direct grants. Additionally, USAID Community Stabilization Programs (CSPs) have historically reduced the incentives for young men to participate in violence, which facilitates security and stabilization. CSPs focus on short-term employment generation through its community infrastructure and essential service projects, which help to deliver basic services at the local level. It then focuses on longer-term job creation through business development programs, providing capital and training to micro, small, and medium-sized private enterprises, particularly those with high employment potential or that have been destroyed by violence. A CSP supports education through its vocational training and apprenticeships that provides employable skills, practical experience, and assistance with job placement in careers such as carpentry, masonry, welding, and sewing. Finally, a CSP focuses on engaging youth through sports, cultural events, skills training, public

service campaigns, and other activities designed to keep young people off the streets and connected in a positive manner with their culture and community.

(3) **US Department of State**. The Bureau for Population, Refugees, and Migration (PRM) supports US and international organizations that provide assistance during humanitarian crises and natural disasters. It has global coverage, and works through providing grants.

(4) **US Department of Commerce (DOC)**. The DOC promotes and develops the foreign and domestic commerce of the United States. It is an extremely large and diverse Department with at least ten operating bureaus, many of which could provide expertise and technical assistance for personnel from a post-conflict country's national government. Commerce has an Office of Reconstruction and Stabilization that can coordinate other expertise in commercial law, customs, export controls, nonproliferation, census, National Oceanographic and Atmospheric Agency (NOAA) expertise and many other areas. Even if not required to deploy in the immediate response, the DOC can provide assistance through reach-back for technical assistance in matters with potential strategic implications. For example, the selection of technologies for cellular telephone service has long-term implications; and DOC's National Telecommunications Information Agency can provide options and advice. In the DOC International Trade Administration (ITA), the Foreign Commercial Service has a global network of trade professionals who promote and protect U.S. commercial interests abroad. ITA has detailed knowledge of local conditions and actors. Additionally, ITA can establish a task force to serve as a clearinghouse of information for companies interested in investing in post conflict environments.

(5) The **US Trade and Development Agency (USTDA)** advances economic development and US commercial interests in developing and middle-income countries. The agency funds various forms of technical assistance, early investment analysis, training, orientation visits and business workshops that support the development of a modern infrastructure and a fair and open trading environment. USTDA gives emphasis to economic sub-sectors that may benefit from US exports of goods and services. Although USTDA does not have immediate response capabilities, technical assistance and grants can be funded in the form of orientation visits, which bring foreign project sponsors to the United States to observe the design, manufacture, demonstration and operation of US products, and services that can potentially help them achieve their development goals.

(6) The **Overseas Private Investment Corporation (OPIC)** mission is to mobilize and facilitate the participation of United States private capital and skills in the economic and social development of less developed countries. OPIC does not have immediate response capabilities, but is well suited to encourage investment in post-crisis nations through reach-back.

(7) The **Export-Import Bank (EX-IM)** assists in financing the export of U.S. goods and services to international markets. The Bank assumes credit and country risks that the private sector is unable or unwilling to accept, which is likely in post-conflict

countries. It provides working capital guarantees (pre-export financing); export credit insurance; and loan guarantees and direct loans (buyer financing).

(8) **US Department of Labor (DOL).** Veterans' Employment and Training Service works on reintegration programs for former military and has expertise with veterans' programs. It operates through grants to contractors and national governments. DOL Bureau of International Labor Affairs, Office of Trade Agreement Administration and Technical Cooperation, provides post-conflict assistance through re-training, reintegrating demobilized soldiers, promoting women's empowerment, educational development of employable skills, etc. for people economically dislocated and victimized by war (e.g., those suffering war-connected disabilities and war widows).

(9) **World Bank Group** (includes the International Financial Corporation) offers funding under various program categories including Conflict Prevention and Reconstruction (the Post-Conflict Fund), infrastructure development, and Low Income Countries Under Stress. The bank provides funding for restoration of lives and livelihoods in postwar environment, small-scale job creation programs, and microfinance projects. Loans and grants are given directly to the UN, national governments, or local NGOs.

(10) **UN**. There are multiple UN organizations supporting livelihood creation programs. These include:

1. The UN Development Program (UNDP) Bureau for Crisis Prevention and Recovery works with civilians to prevent armed conflicts, reduce the risk of disasters, and promote early recovery after crises with grants to NGOs and UN field missions.

2. The UN High Commissioner for Refugees (UNHCR) will fund "quick impact projects" that work with reintegration of returnees and displaced persons through small-scale, low-cost projects, often including income generating and microcredit schemes. Operates through local organizations and self-funded programs wherever there are refugees.

3. The UN Children's Fund provides emergency funds for projects to return child soldiers to civilian life; includes education and training programs.

4. The International Labor Organization (ILO) operates the InFocus program on crisis response and reconstruction that provides technical assistance to promote sustainable employment through capacity building grants to local NGOs and UN field missions. It emphasizes support for women and other vulnerable groups.

8. Develop a Narrative Picture of Employment Needs

Once the necessary data is gathered, planners should develop an analysis or narrative that identifies the current or expected employment situation in the immediate post-crisis period. This should include identifying key needs to be addressed by employment generation programs and a list of notional employment projects to be undertaken. As noted previously, a vital requirement to be addressed in any assessment is how security conditions may affect employment and how joint resources can best be employed to meet this critical need.

9. Implementation Monitoring Measures

a. During the implementation phase, monitoring should focus on what impact employment generation is having on perceived needs and attitudes of the population.

b. Specific measures include:

(1) Indications programs are having or have potential for exacerbating social tensions between groups.

(2) Indications that program benefits are being diverted by potential spoilers.

(3) Potential actions by groups aimed at disrupting initial employment programs, such as labor unions supported by the prior government.

(4) Impact on public attitudes toward the host government, understanding that the goal is to enhance the credibility of the recognized government.

10. Cross References to S/CRS Essential Task Matrix

Appendix B provides the S/CRS Essential Tasks related to the economic sector and supporting infrastructure. Appendix C expands on the activities identified by the S/CRS Essential Tasks Matrix, providing a more detailed list of stability-focused, post-conflict reconstruction essential tasks to help planners identify specific requirements to support countries in transition from armed conflict or civil strife to sustaining stability. It serves as a detailed planning tool.[37] The identification of specific tasks that could potentially contribute to employment generation should be negotiated with the lead US agency and coordinated with the AMEMB country team. Emphasis should be given to anticipating how short-term efforts can be integrated into the overall USG strategy and longer-term reforms and projects.

11. Sub-Sectoral Assessment on Employment Generation

a. The joint planner should access employment generation assessments developed by the USG, partner nations, and international organizations, and apply them to the planning process, as appropriate. The best source for current assessments of the target country will generally be the AMEMB country team. Additionally, the planner should leverage assessments developed by USAID, State S/CRS, MCC and other institutions.

b. Answers to many of the questions needed to assess employment generation activities should be known from conducting the *Comprehensive Assessment* described in Appendix A, Section A. A detailed assessment (Appendix A, Section B) seeks to obtain a comprehensive picture of employment in the area prior to the crisis and how the status quo was affected by the crisis. How did the conflict affect employment and income generating activities? How do other stakeholders currently assess the problem? Of primary concern to the joint force is how employment, and economic activity in general, is being currently affected by the general security situation.

c. Sources of data for this information are the same as for the comprehensive assessment, but a *Tactical Conflict Assessment*[38] can provide more current data that should be shared with civilian agencies and other donors. Any assessment of the employment sub-sector should also include an assessment of how the local population responds to possible incentives and disincentives. Human Terrain Teams, the AMEMB members and intelligence analysts with regional expertise can be helpful in predicting how the local population may respond to possible courses or action. For example, providing technical assistance to the host government as it decides whether to resume operation of a State Owned Enterprise, close it down, or privatize it should be informed by an understanding of how these options might be perceived by the local population. Which groups might benefit from the various options would be an issue to address before choosing a specific option. Restoring operation of an SOE that had unduly benefited from the support of a previously unpopular government could well undercut stabilization efforts while directing support to potential spoiler groups.

CHAPTER III
AGRICULTURE AND FOOD SECURITY

THE MILITARY PROBLEM

In addition to providing a secure environment to process, store, and distribute agricultural products, what are the military supporting tasks, design and planning considerations, and coordination measures required to optimize agricultural production and assist nations in providing food to their populations?

1. Purpose and Scope

Agriculture and food security encompass much more than farm production. Also included are livestock, poultry, grain, vegetables, fruit, fish, fiber, and forestry. Processing of foods, industrial and otherwise, may also be a factor, as will be the production and consumption of forage, and the distribution of agricultural products, foodstuffs, and necessary supporting commodities (e.g., fertilizer, water, fuel, and packaging). Figure III-1 outlines some of the linkages involved in the agriculture value chain and policy environment that USAID and international organizations use for developing long-term agricultural capacity. DOD efforts focus mainly at the services listed at the bottom of the graphic as enablers to support value chain development. During conflict, resulting scarcity of commodities and transportation often results in agricultural activity being reduced to subsistence farming; and trade is often localized, and may involve informal exchanges such as barter. In post-conflict environments, however, agriculture is typically one of the first areas to rebound. Restoring agricultural production and systems needed to get that production to local markets can be undertaken almost immediately post-conflict (or sometimes in the midst of low-intensity conflict) and can provide a primary source of both farm and other employment. Food security issues address availability, access, and use of food by the broader population, including temporary food aid that may be required to bridge food security needs of the population until normal crop production can resume. Humanitarian assistance programs must be finely tuned to avoid degrading local incentives to produce through price and other distortions.

2. Agriculture and Food Security Objectives and Outcomes

a. Secure environment for people, property, and market places.

b. Farmers, fishermen, and others have access to seed, irrigation, fertilizer, extension and veterinary services, equipment, implements, financing, and other related goods and services. Agricultural extension services include application of scientific research and new knowledge to agricultural practices through farmer education, agricultural marketing, health, and business studies.

c. Agricultural market infrastructures are functional: transportation, roads, processing and packinghouses, telecommunication infrastructure required moving goods between production sites, and markets are operable and safe.

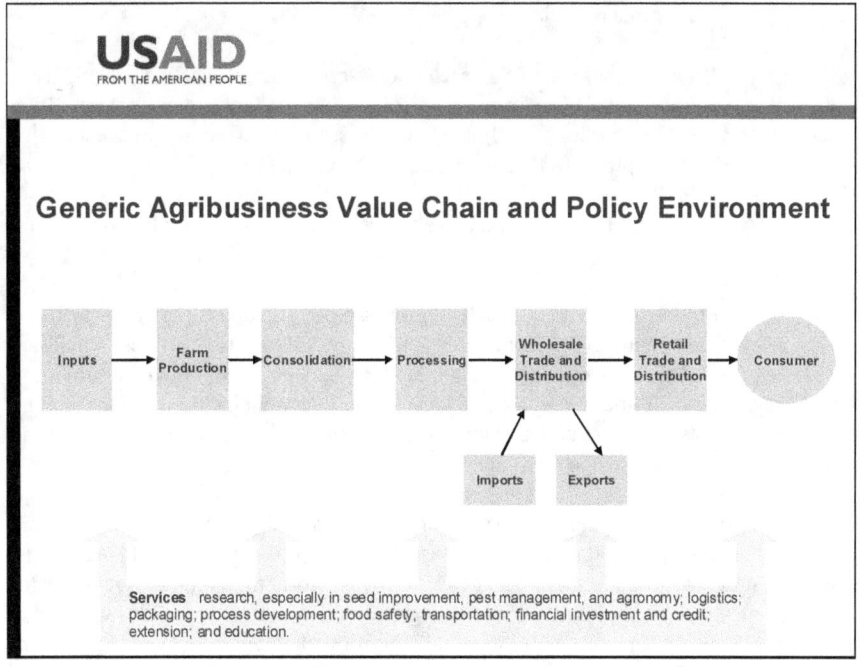

Figure III-1. Generic Agribusiness Value Chain and Policy Environment

d. Minimum level of food availability established through a combination of domestic production, food imports, and humanitarian assistance efforts.

e. Employment opportunities and income support ensures popular access to sufficient food.

3. Agriculture and Food Security Tasks and Planning Considerations

a. A secure and supportive environment for agriculture and food security includes not only the protection of people, property, and marketplaces but also:

(1) Essential services, such as electricity and water, and this may include implementing systematic water allocation to farm, fish, and animal agriculture consumers. Clean water is usually the most important requirement.

(2) Critical private infrastructure such as warehouses, packing sheds, and processing plants.

(3) Key institutional infrastructure that supports agricultural extension services that support food safety, animal health, plant health, and environmental protection.

(4) Safe and open roads (de-mined and cleared) without unauthorized checkpoints.

(5) Basic transportation.

(6) Communications. Cellular telephone service can be established quickly in post-conflict environments. It can be used to decide when to plant and harvest by calling other farmers, to get best prices by calling wholesalers, and to save time by scheduling or meeting deliveries and pick-ups that are infrequently on time.

(7) Financial transaction and credit systems, which could also use cellular telephones.

(8) Private organizations, such as grower, processor, and exporter associations; trade associations; chambers of commerce; etc. Agricultural associations, which are businesses owned and operated by their members, can be encouraged by providing start-up kits. These kits may vary based on local needs, but might include basic agriculture equipment such as a tractor and basic implements to be used by members, or office and communications equipment to facilitate marketing efforts.

b. Transition from humanitarian assistance to self-sustaining production. Food aid has the potential to distort agricultural markets by driving down the price of local goods, discouraging local production, and can conflict with efforts to stimulate private sector development and agricultural employment. Agricultural production recovery and market development can move communities more rapidly from relief dependency to independent livelihood security. It is therefore important to reduce, as soon as is practical, imports of donor food and other relief supplies that can be produced locally.

c. Restarting markets requires simultaneous attention to improving transportation infrastructure, and food production, and instilling confidence in the security environment – at all points in the distribution system – but especially at the point of purchase in the marketplace.

NEW BAGHDAD MARKET

In Iraq, an embedded provincial reconstruction team (PRT) and an Infantry Division's Armor Battalion worked with the Baghdad Provincial Council, local district, and neighborhood councils to establish a modern community-based retail food market. Built with USAID funding in 2004, it was designed for secure shopping, sanitary food handling, and safe food storage; but the market remained unoccupied as violence and ethnic tension drove residents away. Local police continuously ran squatters out of the stalls, and coalition forces often found weapons caches there. In 2008, as stability was established and local residents returned to their neighborhood, hundreds of vendors commandeered nearby streets, not the market, building makeshift stalls to sell vegetables, chicken, and meat. The food market was subsequently opened with improved security and rehabilitated infrastructure.

d. Land access rights and property rights are difficult, and require long-term solutions. In close consultation with the country team, local officials and others should ensure there is an easily accessible, preferably local, process to determine land ownership and resolve disputes.

e. Prepare immediately for the next production and harvest season by encouraging development of market-based systems to provide necessary inputs for crop sowing and as well as support systems needed to gather, market and distribute the harvest.

(1) If the effort begins before the planting season, help returning farmers begin family gardens, subsistence farming, and cash cropping by facilitating local venues where farmers can buy or exchange local seeds directly with other farmers (called seed fairs), and provide vouchers and start-up kits of tools.

(2) If returning refugees and Internally-Displaced Persons (IDPs) arrive late in the planting season, be prepared to support these households with humanitarian assistance until the following harvest period.

f. Identify available sources of required expertise; and start planning for long-term recovery right away. Participate actively with the country team in their coordination efforts with the local government, donors, NGOs, and local farmers knowledgeable about the local environment. Establish a CMOC, if required.

NATIONAL GUARD

A Tennessee Army National Guard Agribusiness Development Team deployed for a year to Afghanistan to assist farmers in that region. The team is composed of soldiers with a wide variety of Military Occupational Skills from throughout Tennessee. The soldiers, accompanied by a security team, are prepared to teach basic farming techniques such as planting and harvesting wheat, planting corn in rows, and using trellises to grow tomatoes and grapes. They can also work to improve irrigation systems and crop storage facilities. The objective is to help farmers in Afghanistan become more self-sufficient, while avoiding the illegal drug trade.

---

g. The first steps toward generating agricultural employment should emphasize job opportunities that help put unused agricultural land back into production. Beginning with the country's major agricultural production areas, target rural communities and farms for assistance. Because of the typical lag in the rebound of private investment in farming, public financing and assistance projects may be needed for such tasks as rebuilding warehousing and feeder roads, and repairing water delivery systems. Investment decisions should be based on both how effective they would be in bringing land back under cultivation and providing jobs and increasing productivity. In some instances increasing land under cultivation will be a good decision, even if the economic efficiency might prove to be marginal.

A Rural Finance Leaders Development Program (RFLD) was managed through the US Department of Agriculture's (USDA) Agribusiness Development and Policy Support Project (ADAPS) and financed by USAID. Iowa State University (ISU) worked with USDA to design and implement the RFLD program for Romania. The project provided team-building and technical assistance with the aim to improve credit access in rural regions of Romania. The project created a team of people able to assist the farmers and agribusinesses in accessing credit from Commercial Banks. A pilot program provided small agribusinesses with the tools needed to access credit, created relationships with both private and public consultants and help them understand how to develop a business plan for small agribusinesses, and contacted local banks and other financers to understand the changes taking place within the sector, and the credit products available to farmers.

h. Assess the capability of local government, facilitate technical assistance, and support socio-economic and agricultural institution-building, including extension and education services through USDA's FAS, USAID or via reachback.

A PRT leader in Iraq coordinated with the Brigade Commander, who used CERP funds to install computer, audio, and video equipment that facilitated the reach-back from an Iraqi University to a US Land Grant University. Initially used for information and technical exchanges, the system now allows distance-learning between universities.

i. Provide emergency veterinary services for both animal health and food safety. US Army Veterinary personnel can provide emergency services and build local partnerships.

j. Develop a Communication Strategy. Public perceptions, confidence, and other effects in the cognitive dimension directly affect agriculture and food security. Informing, educating, and convincing the local population to support agricultural programs that are beneficial to them can be a challenge. A communication strategy should integrate all communication capability, such as public affairs, information operations, and defense support to public diplomacy. Likewise, the communication strategy should leverage all communications means and methods that are effective in the local environment. To achieve an effective synchronization of words, images and actions requires communication strategy integration into all planning, execution, and assessment activities. For more information, see the JWFC *Commander's Handbook for Strategic Communication and Communication Strategy*, version 2.0, 27 October 2009, at the following link: http://www.dtic mil/doctrine/doctrine/jwfc_pam.htm.

4. Key Interagency Partners and Coordination Processes for Agriculture and Food Security

a. The AMEMB country team is the principal for planning and coordination. The country team will generally have at least one economic officer, representatives of the

USAID, and possibly from the Departments of Commerce, Treasury, Agriculture and others. These officials will be the best positioned to advise the joint force on the current situation as well as programs sponsored by the host government, the USG, and other donors. All these offices receive support from their respective Washington-based headquarters, as described below.

b. USAID is the main partner in the field for the joint force. USAID's OFDA deploys Disaster Assistance Response Teams that provide an immediate, on-the-ground, assessment, and work routinely with other organizations that are providing humanitarian assistance in fragile states and in post-disaster environments. OTI works with civilians in fragile states using quick impact projects lasting 2-3 years. The Conflict Mitigation Office and Economic Growth Bureau also support initiatives. All operate through contracts to implementing partners/NGOs and direct grants. USAID can also fund the post-conflict operations of USDA and other Departments.

c. **USDA.** The USDA FAS offers a wide range of technical assistance, education, and outreach programs for emerging agricultural markets and developing countries, that are designed to support the development of science-based regulatory policies and promote food security. Some of the activities include: **agricultural trade capacity building, agricultural development resources and disaster assistance, food assistance, promoting agricultural trade and investment, international development job opportunities in agriculture, agricultural trade and scientific exchanges, Cochran Fellowship Program in Agriculture, and the Norman E. Borlaug International Agricultural Science and Technology Fellows Program.** USDA experts have served as provincial reconstruction team (PRT) agricultural advisors in Afghanistan and Iraq.

d. **International Organizations**. Members of the international community, such as the World Bank, several United Nation agencies, regional development banks, and other bilateral donors and NGOs, may also be able to provide resources. Joint Force interface with these institutions should use existing coordination mechanisms, such as USAID and USDA, who coordinate with these organizations, US universities, and/or other US and international organizations to facilitate cooperation on international food, science, and technology issues. They include **the International Fund for Agricultural Development (IFAD), Food and Agriculture Organization of the UN (FAO), Organization for Economic Cooperation and Development (OECD), World Food Programme (WFP), Inter-American Institute for Cooperation on Agriculture (IICA), World Bank, and Inter-American Development Bank**.

e. The USG can provide food aid through direct donations and concessional programs, using four program authorities listed below. The US Agency for International Development (USAID) administers Public Law 480, Title II Emergency and Private Assistance program. USDA administers the other food aid programs and the Bill Emerson Humanitarian Trust.

f. The USAID Administered Public Law 480, Title II–Emergency and Private Assistance, provides for the donation of US agricultural commodities to meet emergency and nonemergency food needs in countries, including support for food security goals. However, agricultural commodities donated by the USG to meet emergency needs are traditionally provided through the World Food Program (WFP) or Private Volunteer Organizations (PVOs).

g. The Food for Progress (FFP) program provides for the donation or credit sale of US commodities to developing countries and emerging democracies to support democracy and an expansion of private enterprise. To date, all food aid under this program has been by donation. USDA also uses FFP to target countries in transition, and focus on private sector development of agricultural sub-sectors such as improved agricultural techniques, marketing systems, farmer education and cooperative development, expanded use of processing capacity, and development of agriculturally related businesses. For example, the FFP agreement between USDA and National Rural Electric Cooperative Association (NRECA) provided $8.5 million in commodities for use in the Philippines. NRECA sold the commodities, and used the funds to help establish and finance the Rural Electric Finance Corporation of the Philippines (REFC). Once established, the REFC financed a lending program. Loan projects included power distribution improvements and expansion, small power supply projects, and renewable energy systems. As a result, 120 electric co-ops in the Philippines provide as many as 5 million people with electricity every day.

h. The McGovern-Dole International Food for Education Program and Child Nutrition Program[39] helps support education, child development, and food security for some of the world's poorest children. It provides for donations of US agricultural products, financial and technical assistance, schoolchildren feeding and maternal and child nutrition projects in low-income, food-deficient countries that are committed to universal education.

i. The Section 416(b) program provides for overseas donations of surplus commodities; however, it is currently inactive due to the unavailability of government-owned commodities.

j. The Bill Emerson Humanitarian Trust is another important resource to ensure that the USG can respond to emergency food aid needs. The Emerson Trust is not a food aid program, but a food reserve, administered under the authority of the Secretary of Agriculture. US commodities from this reserve can be used to respond to humanitarian food crises in developing countries, particularly those that emerge unexpectedly. Up to 4 million metric tons of US wheat, corn, sorghum, and rice can be kept in its reserve. The Secretary of Agriculture is authorized to release commodities from the Emerson Trust to provide food aid for emergency needs that cannot otherwise be met through Public Law 480.

k. The interagency Food Assistance Policy Council, chaired by USDA's Under Secretary for Farm and Foreign Agricultural Services, is one of the USG coordination mechanisms for US food aid policies and programs. The council includes representatives from the Office of Management and Budget (OMB), the Department of State, USAID, and USDA.

5. Case Studies from USAID "A Guide to Economic Growth in Post-Conflict Countries"

a. Jump-Starting Wartime Markets in Southern Sudan

(1) A variety of programs successfully jump-started local market economies in southern Sudan during the waning years of conflict and in the post-conflict years. These initiatives helped re-establish the business capacities of farmers, traders, and transporters. Evolving during years of unusual and changing circumstances, these initiatives made it possible for currency to circulate and for trade goods to reach nearly all corners of southern Sudan.

(2) Historically, southern Sudan has been underdeveloped, has not had market traditions, and has used a barter system of exchange. Most southern Sudanese did not handle cash and had no access to markets. During the war years in particular, markets were limited primarily to garrison towns. All goods arrived on military flights from Khartoum and were sold mainly to Sudanese government employees. Prices were greatly distorted; and markets had few linkages with the surrounding countryside.

(3) When humanitarian NGOs began relief operations in the early 1990s, their workers were paid in soap and salt because cash held no value in rural areas. After the SPLA captured some of the major towns in Western Equatorial in the mid to late 1990s, things started to change. OFDA-funded NGO programs began to open up isolated areas and stimulate local economies. NGO recovery programs initially focused on barter and agriculture, airlifting basic consumer items (such as salt, soap, blankets, buckets, and bicycles) to major towns, and then exchanging those items for seed and surplus grain grown by local farmers. The seeds and grain were subsequently sold to NGOs carrying out relief operations elsewhere in Southern Sudan. Over time, barter exchanges gave way to cash transactions that helped establish the "right" price relationships. One USAID approach to developing cash markets involved selling US emergency food-aid wheat in Uganda, and using the Ugandan shilling proceeds to buy local grain in Southern Sudan. This program subsequently expanded into other market-supporting activities.

(4) In later years, locally initiated "peace committees" set up eight "peace markets" in greater Bahr el Ghazal. These markets enabled northerners and southerners to put aside their political and social differences and exchange consumer goods and livestock in relative security. The peace committees negotiated rules for the peace markets, such as a prohibition on weapons within designated market areas. The peace markets enjoyed several years of relative success in the years immediately preceding the Comprehensive Peace Agreement of December 2004; because each side perceived benefits from continued trade.

(5) Key lessons learned from the programs in Southern Sudan include:

(a) Revitalizing farmer cooperatives can increase the effectiveness of local grain purchases by helping amass grain from individual farmers, resulting in savings for purchasers and higher unit prices for farmers.

(b) Encouraging surplus food production is unsustainable without steady market demand, even when stimulated by NGOs during emergency and transition phases.

(c) Restarting markets requires simultaneous attention to improving roads that reduce transport costs, increase volumes, and lower prices.

b. Seed vouchers and seed fairs are often better than direct distribution.

(1) Both seed fairs (local venues where farmers can buy or exchange local seeds directly with other farmers) and seed vouchers connect farmers who have seeds to barter or sell with those who need them. Seed sales increase the income of the sellers, who are usually farmers themselves, and are often women. Experience shows that prices are generally within expected market ranges. Seed sales also can have a positive multiplier effect on the local economy. Unlike direct seed distribution to passive recipients, these alternative approaches empower farming households, providing them with opportunities to make their own choices.

> *"The military is giving away free wheat seed to Afghan farmers, and that's undermining our efforts, said an expert whose USAID-supported program gave farmers vouchers to buy seeds, which was helping build a secondary market of seed- and farm-supply businesses."*
>
> **Chairman of the Joint Chiefs of Staff,**
> **Reporting on a visit to Afghanistan in 2009**
> **Joe Klein, "Diplomatic Surge: Can Obama's Team Tame the Taliban?"**
> **Time.com, 4/9/2009**

(2) Knowledgeable farmers are able to distinguish among local seed varieties to obtain desired seed characteristics. These farmers are unlikely to plant newly introduced outside seed until they personally have grown it and gauged its performance. For this reason, farmers overwhelmingly prefer their own seed varieties, and will save them even in years of crisis, supplementing their supply through barter or purchase. In post-conflict settings, most seed is likely to come from these informal arrangements, which vary by crop and region. Except in cases of widespread or prolonged conflict, it is a mistake to assume that production failure necessarily equates to seed scarcity.

(3) Outside seeds distributed for post-conflict recovery often are unsuitable to local conditions and fail. The most effective—and hence, most helpful—seed-distribution systems supply seeds that farmers have problems acquiring. The best source of such seeds is through the extant farmer seed system itself.

(4) Recognizing that donor grant-distribution of seeds may undermine farmer seed systems and local markets, more and more international relief agencies and NGOs are experimenting with seed fairs where farmers can buy or exchange local seeds directly with other farmers. These seed varieties are time-tested, adapted to local growing conditions, and well-known. Farmer reputation is the most critical guarantee of quality.

Another recovery option is the use of vouchers distributed by sponsoring NGOs to targeted households. The households can "spend" the face value of their vouchers at participating retail outlets for the seeds of their choice (usually local-variety, farmer-saved seed) to jump-start the system.

(5) The use of local seeds requires a "seed security assessment" to ascertain:

(a) That seed-source households in the area have sufficient seeds (availability).

(b) That these seeds are safely stored and acceptable for the next growing season (quality).

(c) That the seed-source households are able to meet their own needs before selling or bartering their seeds (sustainability), and that needy households have the means to buy or barter for seeds (access).

c. Equally important as the distribution of seeds is the technical expertise required to select the seed. Undertaking seed distribution without the requisite expertise may result in distributing seed unsuitable for the region, and could actually turn the population against joint forces.

6. Suggested Monitoring Measures

a. Does the security environment restrict the free movement of people, goods, and services related to agriculture and food security?

b. Do environmental causes of drought or lack of water, pest invasions, and infectious animal disease threaten food security?

c. Do land ownership issues inhibit crop or animal production or promote conflicts? Are there significant tracts of land lying fallow due to questions over ownership?

d. Use cross-references to the Department of State Essential Task Matrix. Appendix C expands on the activities identified by the S/CRS Essential Tasks Matrix. The identification of specific joint tasks that could potentially contribute to agriculture and food security must be negotiated with the lead US agency and coordinated with the AMEMB country team. Emphasis should be given to anticipating how short-term efforts can be integrated into the overall USG strategy and longer-term reforms and projects.

7. Sub Sectoral Assessment on Agriculture

a. In most economies, the agricultural sub-sector will be an integral part of the national economy, as a major employer, a supplier of essential foodstuffs and raw material for local industry, and a foreign export earner. An assessment of the agricultural sub-sector usually carried out by civilian experts from or contracted by State, USAID, and/or

USDA, will provide a baseline for planning desired short and intermediate term outcomes that support strategic objectives.

b. The assessment should provide an accurate picture of agriculture's role in the national and regional economy, and continue with a more detailed assessment of the elements in the food security value chain. These include key products, key inputs required to sustain agricultural production, and key issues that affect efficient operation of the value chains. Among the areas examined are informal enterprise and market development, informal cross border trading, opportunities to reinvigorate microenterprise development, and opportunities to restore basic agriculture skill levels and infrastructure. The assessment will identify short-term agriculture policies required to transition from efforts to restore agricultural production to pre-crisis levels to longer-term policies promoting further growth and development. The focus, however, should remain on the basic inputs of agriculture — land, labor, and capital. An outline of an agricultural sub-sector assessment is provided in Appendix A, Section C.

c. For many developing economies with a significant agriculture sub-sector, an assessment may already be available from USAID, USDA, or a similar development institution. If not, the best sources of this information are the Food and Agriculture Organization of the UN (FAO),[40] the Economic Research Service of USDA,[41] and the Economist Intelligence Unit,[42] and the references it lists.

Intentionally Blank

Military Support To Economic Stabilization

CHAPTER IV
GOVERNMENT FINANCE, CENTRAL BANK, PRIVATE BANKING, AND FINANCIAL SUB-SECTOR

THE MILITARY PROBLEM

How does a joint force commander support stabilization of public and private financial systems in support of mission objectives?

1. Scope

a. Stabilizing the financial sub-sector of a country following conflict involves working with three interrelated components:

(1) Getting the macroeconomic fundamentals right. Government financial institutions, normally centered in a ministry of finance, need to be able to establish and implement a national budget that balances central government expenditures, including payments to security forces and ex-combatants, with government revenues, foreign donor contributions, and government external borrowing. Securing adequate funding for government to finance essential public goods and services will be a critical challenge. Since mechanisms to collect taxes will usually be weak or nonexistent in a post-conflict economy. Customs duties and royalties from the exploitation of natural resource will generally be the main revenue sources. A national budget that limits government deficits and creates a sustainable fiscal position will help restrain inflation, and is a prerequisite for balance of payments support and reconstruction assistance from the International Monetary Fund (IMF) and the World Bank.

(2) Re-establishing the basic functions of the central bank or similar government institution that manages the country's money supply, controls credit, and supports the operations of domestic private banks. The central bank is responsible for formulating and implementing a country's monetary policy to ensure the stability of the national currency. It provides credibility and support to banks so they are viewed as trustworthy, and can sometimes make payments for governments, acting as the government's bank.

(3) Restoring commercial bank operations to provide individuals and businesses a safe means for saving, making payments to others, and providing loans for business and personal consumption.

b. The operation of the financial sub-sector is highly specialized. Once undermined by conflict or crisis, recovery requires an integrated strategy that takes a comprehensive approach to restoring the sub-sector. Normally, this is a function of civilian agencies, with international financial institutions (IFIs), such as the International Monetary Fund and the World Bank, and individual government donors generally take the lead. Within the USG, this is a function of the Department of Treasury.

c. Any military roles must be taken with an understanding of USG objectives and strategic guidance. The Departments of Treasury and State engage with foreign governments, the IFIs, and other multilateral groups to assess country conditions, develop policies, and define objectives for countries. From the assessment in Appendix A, Joint forces should be prepared to support the specific objectives and programs supported by the USG and its international partners in the banking and finance sub-sector. Essential elements of a basic financial recovery program may include:

(1) Stabilizing the country's currency;

(2) Securing sources and means of government revenue and establishing a national budget;

(3) Establishing a system for domestic and international funds transfers;

(4) Facilitating the establishment and regulation of a private banking and financial system that meets the country's needs;

(5) Facilitating business credit at the community level; and

(6) Establishing and enforcing a body of regulatory and accounting standards that ensures the security of the financial system from fraud and mismanagement.

d. In addition to its role in establishing policy and strategic objectives, the Department of Treasury has a cadre of technical assistance advisors with specialized expertise who embed with host nation officials to implement policies. USAID also provides specialized expertise in banking and financial assistance, and can fund additional medium- and long-term technical assistance programs.

e. Immediate joint support to USG efforts centers on coordination through the Joint Staff and OSD, using existing mechanisms. This coordination with other USG Departments, IFIs, other international governmental organizations, and International Banks is used to understand the country's systems, provide security to a country's physical and financial infrastructure, and conduct tactical fiscal operations in the country to minimize the impact of introducing joint forces and external currencies on both the financial sub-sector and the economy at large.[43] In cases where hostilities preclude the operation of civilian donor agencies, US joint forces may also be needed, on a limited basis, to help restore financial operations directly, most likely at a community level.

2. Operational Relevance and Objectives

a. Banking and finance are the lifeblood of commerce. The speed at which the banking and financial sub-sector are stabilized directly impacts economic activity and employment, and may influence popular support for a government.

b. The objectives related to the banking and finance sub-sector includes:

(1) Government financial leaders, institutions, assets, and records are physically secure.

(2) Secure banks and nonbank institutions are available to the population and to businesses to provide basic financial services at the community level. This includes accepting deposits, making loans, providing a means to transfer funds within the country, as well as internationally.

(3) The government is effectively implementing a sustainable national budget; and if applicable, holds the government deficit within agreed IMF and World Bank limits. The government is collecting revenue, making payments to government employees and pensioners, and has the capability to manage government finances.

(4) Exchange rate is stable, and inflation is brought under control.

(5) Commercial loans and other financial services are increasingly available at the community level, in secondary cities and rural areas, offsetting the need for foreign donor agencies to engage in making loans and grants.

(6) Hostile forces and criminal elements are effectively locked out of making illicit financial transfers through the banking system.

(7) Private banking and financial institutions are subject to government prudential regulation and audit, but are otherwise unconstrained to conduct financial activities both within the country and with institutions abroad without unwarranted government interference.

(8) Regulated electronic payments systems are emerging to supplement the cash economy.

3. Essential Tasks and Planning Considerations

a. **Securing and Protecting Government Assets**. In many countries, governments will have stockpiles of liquid assets, such as gold and stocks of foreign and domestic currency. Planners should anticipate operations to locate and secure such assets to prevent theft or looting. Procedures should also be established for securing and inventorying stocks of currency, high-value commodities, and financial records.

b. **Securing and Protecting Key Government Financial Infrastructure**. Equally important as the physical structures identified as protected targets, are the people in leadership positions in the central and large private banks, and related information technology (IT) hardware and software (including the software programmers and maintenance personnel). Often overlooked, IT and supporting telecommunications are the lifeblood of a banking system; and early consideration of their safeguarding is important. The Department of Treasury and Federal Reserve, and sometimes large private commercial banks, may be able to provide a list of the critical facilities, assets, and information that would have to be located and secured in order to make it possible for monetary authorities of a successor government or occupation authority to take effective control of the money supply and regulate the financial sub-sector as quickly as possible. That list might include:

(1) The system software developers;

(2) The internal accounting systems;

(3) The legal document systems;

(4) The clearinghouse information systems;

(5) The key nationals within the central bank who are most knowledgeable about the workings of the systems;

(6) The personnel of private foreign banks, foreign central banks, IMF, World Bank, and other organizations that have extensive interactions with the personnel and information systems in the HN;

(7) The personnel and computer systems of large commercial banks in the HN; and

(8) Key telecommunications facilities and systems.

c. **Providing Secure Logistical Support**. To finance large-scale operations, Joint forces should be prepared to provide logistical support to the movement of significant amounts of US currency to the host country. During the US occupation of Iraq, occupation authorities shipped $12 billion of vested Iraqi funds, weighing 237.3 tons, to Iraq over a 12-month period. This was used to pay the salaries of Iraqi government officials and for reconstruction projects. If host government authorities introduce a new currency, it will typically be printed abroad, and need to be transported to the country and distributed by as secure a means as possible. Joint forces should be prepared to provide such logistical and security support. In Iraq, US authorities carried out the exchange of old for new Iraqi dinars, with armed convoys delivering new Iraqi dinars to 243 banks across the country, between October 2003 and January 2004.

d. **Strategy and Coordination for Short-Term Macroeconomic Stability**. Supporting the stabilization of banking and the financial sub-sector in many cases will require an agreed-upon long-term strategy and a high degree of coordination with the activities of non-US international organizations. While the United States is generally an important donor country, host government financial policies will be largely influenced by the IMF and the World Bank. The advice of these institutions has a major influence on a government's policies with respect to inflation, fiscal stability, financial sub-sector regulation, and the country's ability to finance debt. IFI's are also a major source of assistance designed to strengthen a country's administrative and institutional capacity. For example, in the first 18 months after the 2003 invasion of Iraq, the IMF's Emergency Post-conflict Assistance (EPCA) program provided technical assistance and training to Iraqi officials in matters related to tax policy, budget preparation and execution, central banking, the creation of a treasury bill market, and collection of statistics. In concert with OSD and the Joint Staff, Joint forces should maintain awareness of IMF and central bank plans, so military activities do not interfere or conflict.

e. **Basic Financial Management Functions**. The host nation must be able to perform certain basic financial management functions. The Joint force must understand, support, and be prepared to initially conduct these functions:

(1) **Government Revenue**. The host government must be able to collect revenue to operate. If a government's tax and customs administrations have collapsed, expatriate personnel may be called upon to assist government officials to re-establish essential fiscal and financial functions. In rare cases, Joint forces should be prepared to support the government in receiving and accounting for revenue. For example, customs duties on imports and royalties on natural resource exports are frequently the main sources of revenue. Collection of these duties and royalties, in turn, requires secure borders, including seaports and airports, and the participation of civilian agencies that can help the country's authorities build their capability to collect customs duties and other taxes. The Department of Treasury, USAID, and the Department of Homeland Security Customs and Border Patrol (CBP) and Immigration and Customs Enforcement (ICE) can also provide this kind of technical assistance.

(2) **Government Budget**. A government's legitimacy with the population will largely depend on its ability to operate and deliver essential goods services. One of the top economic challenges to a post-conflict government is to formulate a national budget that funds essential government services within a resource envelope that includes local revenue sources and donor financing, and does not require issuance of large amounts of debt that could spark inflation and undermine the currency. The World Bank, USAID, and other foreign government development agencies provide technical advice and support to governments in the establishment of a national budget. Joint forces can support such efforts to share their assessments of public facilities and services with host country authorities and donors, and participate in prioritization of public investment needs. This prioritization of budgetary requirements should also include requirements of host country security forces, any DDR or similar programs involving the security sector, and infrastructure that is critical to maintaining security. If the situation requires, joint forces should be prepared to advise the host country government on program prioritization, budget expenditures, and management of payments to host country security forces, former combatants, government employees, pensioners, social services, etc.

(3) **Government Payment Mechanisms and Revenue Disbursement**. The government must be able to disburse pensions and other social safety net resources. If electronic mechanisms do not exist, cash transactions will be required, and may need joint force support to secure, transport, and distribute cash instruments.

f. **Banks**. There may have been a pre-conflict run on banks; and local banks may be closed, insolvent, or simply not trusted. The effects and implications of this are:

(1) Local currency may not be available; and joint forces may have to bring currency for payment to locals for services.

(2) Joint forces may be requested to provide logistics or security support to the Central Bank, or similar entity, that is responsible for issuing currency, chartering

banks, insuring deposits, facilitating the availability of credit, and general controlling the availability of credit and the country's money supply.

(3) Support to banking must include an understanding of legacy banking systems and associated property rights. The Department of Treasury Regional desk officer and Office of Technical Assistance usually have established long-standing relationships and knowledge of legacy systems.

(4) The best anti-corruption practice is auditing. The Departments of Treasury and State, the Financial Services Volunteer Corps, and USAID can sponsor the US Federal Deposit Insurance Corporation, and other organizations, to provide technical assistance in bank auditing.

(5) Informal banking systems used for money transfer and the delivery of remittances may be the only system in place. In many developing or traditional economies, small informal money and foreign exchange dealers, such as hawalas or black market peso exchanges, meet the financial service needs of communities, instead of formal banks. They transfer remittances from migrant workers and exchange currency. Joint forces should generally avoid interfering with hawalas and other informal financial institutions, and try to legitimize, rather than drive out of business, small foreign exchange dealers. Due to the highly competitive nature of small markets, they may provide such services to the community at lower cost, and employ a larger number of people than formal financial institutions. However, because informal systems don't have formal records of transactions, they may be used for illicit funds transfers, including criminal and terrorist networks. Nonetheless, in light of their importance to communities, joint forces should give first priority to providing ways to legitimize the informal systems by supporting limited host government regulation, rather than prohibit them and rely on law enforcement and other security mechanisms to combat illicit transfers.

(6) An informal and many times criminal economy may be present in a post-conflict environment. Joint forces should plan to share information and intelligence, establish structures, and build capabilities to exploit and counter illicit financial networks. The Department of Treasury Office of Terrorism and Financial Intelligence is the primary USG partner with this expertise; and their participation should be solicited in establishing a Counter-Threat Finance organization. The effectiveness of these efforts increases if the host government is a viable partner.

(7) In situations when security conditions limit commercial loans or donor grant/loan activity for small business, joint forces may, in the short-term, fill the financing gap through bulk funded direct micro-grants and facilitating microfinance by connecting those in need with the appropriate agencies and organizations conducting microfinance programs. Bulk funding for direct micro-grants can be provided through various contingency fund sources, such as the (commander's emergency response program (CERP)).[44] Although there may be few banks willing to provide loans, there are many microfinance institutions willing to provide capital to small businesses, and numerous charitable groups and websites who link investors to poor borrowers. Successful micro finance operations require attributes that are not well suited to joint forces. They require constant and sustained contact with borrowers. They also require substantial technical

assistance to the providers. Joint forces may become a facilitator between the population and institutions that can provide micro-finance by establishing financial service technology centers. USAID has extensive experience in microfinance, and should be the first source to assist and provide additional planning considerations. The World Bank has also done extensive research on microfinance.

WHAT IS MICROFINANCE?

Microfinance is the extension of very small business loans (without requiring collateral) to persons who are unemployed or impoverished. The concept is based on the highly successful Grameen Bank Project (from the Bengali word for "village") in the mid 1970s, that initially made loans averaging $27 to 42 families so they could produce small items without the burden of predatory financing. In its present-day form, microfinance is typically provided by local community banks, or similar institutions set up by donor development agencies. These local institutions make small loans in amounts up to several thousand dollars to develop small businesses, frequently operated by women, in rural areas of developing countries. By basing the promise of repayment on personal and family honor rather than formal collateral, Grameen-style banking generally has high rates of repayment and generates business activity in areas where commercial banks are unwilling or unable to operate. Given their widespread acceptance as a development tool, USAID and other foreign donor agencies may consider establishing microfinance initiatives to stimulate economic growth, taking care to separate microfinance initiatives from grant programs that develop small businesses. Donor agencies recognize that microfinance initiatives are not a substitute for reconstituting a country's core banking capacity; and these initiatives should supplement a much broader financial sector assistance program.

---

g. **Small and Medium Enterprises (SMEs)**. Microfinance has proven very effective, and helps individuals. However, it does not have the larger and more economically stimulating effects of financing to SMEs. Joint forces should support the Department of Treasury and USAID, who work with banks to do credit analysis of borrowers, and provide high risk lending.

h. **Stable Currency, Inflation and Minimizing the Impact of Military Spending on the Local Economy**. A stable and growing economy requires low inflation, and keeping people's purchasing power stable. Conflict, large budgetary deficits, lack of public confidence in the government, and other factors may add to inflation, causing residents to flee from the national currency and convert their funds to dollars, Euros, or other currencies. The mere presence of the joint force will also directly and immediately affect the local economy. Without careful planning, this joint force increase on demand may increase inflationary pressure. To maximize the positive effect on the economy, forces should purchase goods and services on the local economy, if purchases do not create local shortages that hurt the local population. If necessary, programs to augment local supplies of key goods should be identified in coordination with the national government and foreign donors. To minimize the effect on inflation, joint forces should make all payments for goods and services in the local currency, pay wages for local services at an appropriate wage-rate, and ensure prices paid for local goods are not inflated. When present, the UN can research local conditions and recommend an appropriate wage rate for use by all donors. Although it is generally more convenient to use dollars, using the local currency helps put useable cash in the hands of the populace, stimulates the economy, and demonstrates confidence in the country's government. It is a concrete action reinforcing the strategic message that joint forces are engaged with the populace; and it avoids aggravating any local tensions between the "haves"—persons with access to US dollar-denominated payments—and "have-nots". How to re-establish that confidence and avoid "dollarizing" the economy is a challenge best addressed by US Treasury, USAID, and the WB and IMF. The military should follow their advice on how to manage its financial affairs in country. Finally, joint forces should use and encourage electronic payment systems going directly to the individual (to the extent feasible), to discourage embezzlement and corruption.

i. **Develop a Communication Strategy**. Public perceptions, trust, confidence, and other effects in the cognitive dimension directly affect the financial sub-sector. A communication strategy should integrate all communication capability, such as public affairs, information operations, and defense support to public diplomacy to inform and educate the local populace and garner support for our activities. The communication strategy should leverage all communications means and methods that are effective in the local environment. To achieve an effective synchronization of words, images and actions requires communication strategy integration into all planning, execution, and assessment activities. For more information, see the JWFC *Commander's Handbook for Strategic Communication and Communication Strategy*, version 2.0, 27 October 2009, at the following link: http://www.dtic mil/doctrine/doctrine/jwfc_pam.htm.

4. Key Interagency Partners and Coordination Processes

a. The **AMEMB country team** is the principal for planning and coordination. It will generally have at least one economic officer, representatives of USAID, and possibly from the Departments of Commerce, Treasury, Agriculture and others. These officials will be the best positioned to advise the joint force on the current situation, as well as programs already sponsored by the host government, the USG, and other donors. All these offices receive support from their respective Washington-based headquarters, as described below.

b. **USAID**. Many offices support the country team, including the Democracy Conflict and Humanitarian Assistance (DCHA) Office of Transition Initiatives (OTI), and several offices within the Economic Growth Agriculture and Trade (EGAT) Bureau. USAID has experience providing development assistance in fiscal infrastructure, monetary policy, and central and commercial banking.

c. **US Treasury Department**. Two offices within Treasury lead parts of the effort:

(1) For the Under Secretary for International Affairs, the Office of Regional/Country Affairs represents the USG in International Financial Institutions and provides Treasury with attaches who work locally with foreign governments and IFIs to develop

policy. The Office of Technical Assistance provides the cadre of technical advisors who can deploy to the ministry of finance and the central bank.

(2) For the Under Secretary for Terrorism and Financial Intelligence, the Office of Foreign Asset Control and the Office of Terrorist Financing and Financial Crimes work with the country and international community to combat money laundering and other financial crimes. They administer and enforce economic and trade sanctions against specific foreign countries and regimes, terrorists, international narcotics traffickers, those engaged in activities related to the proliferation of weapons of mass destruction, and other threats.

d. **World Bank Group** (including the International Financial Corporation) offers funding under various program categories. These include Conflict Prevention and Reconstruction (the Post-Conflict Fund), the Infrastructure Development Program, and the Low Income Countries under Stress Program. The World Bank also provides loans and grants to the UN, national governments, or local nongovernmental organizations, that can support microfinance projects and funding for restoration of lives and livelihoods in a postwar environment. Joint forces should engage the World Bank through the country team, OSD, the Joint Staff, and Treasury Department.

e. The **International Monetary Fund** has multiple programs that can provide balance of payment support, as well as offering technical assistance for finance ministry and central bank operations.

f. **Commercial Banks**. Based on historical ties with the HN, large international commercial banks may have operations in developing countries, or desire to quickly establish/restart them. They may be sources of valuable information, and are best approached through the country team.

5. Implementation Monitoring Measures

a. An attack on senior government or prominent commercial financial personnel, financial institutions, records, communications, information technology systems, or assets.

b. Insolvency or a run on a major bank.

c. Criminal money laundering or financial transfers that support hostile forces or terrorist organizations.

d. Changes in the inflow of remittances from the country's expatriate community, and the reason.

6. Cross References to S/CRS Essential Task Matrix

Appendix C expands on the activities identified by the S/CRS Essential Task Matrix. The identification of specific tasks that could potentially contribute to banking and finance should be negotiated with the lead US agency and coordinated with the AMEMB country team. Emphasis should be given to anticipating how short-term efforts can be integrated into the overall USG strategy and longer-term reforms and projects.

7. Sub-Sectoral Assessment on Finance

The comprehensive assessment from Appendix A, Section A, is generally all that is required; however, ensure that assessments from the DOT, DOS, IMF, and World Bank are available. Appendix A, Section D, identifies specific information from the general assessment and additional information that may be needed.

APPENDIX A
ASSESSMENTS

SECTION A. ASSESSING A POST-CONFLICT ECONOMY

1. Overview of a Post-Conflict Economic Assessment

a. Each country has a unique economic structure based on its resources, the needs of the people, laws, customs, traditions, and level of development. The four steps performed in a standard assessment are designed to support the planning processes, and the development of economic goals, measures, and general courses of action, specifying who, what, when, where and why economic actions are to be taken. The assessment should describe the situation, desired end state, commander's intent, and strategic objectives (interagency major mission elements) to stabilize a post-conflict economy, reduce the economic drivers of conflict, and increase institutional capacity.

b. The **four steps** in conducting an economic assessment are:

(1) **Compile a country economic profile** to understand the policy, strategy, environment, and performance of the economy. This establishes "baseline" conditions, and identifies problems inhibiting growth of the economy. In addition to providing key economic data, the profile should include the country's economic strategy, macro-economic performance, dominant economic sub-sectors (e.g., agriculture energy, raw materials production), key micro-economic/sub-sector policies affecting private sector business, social policies (health, education, and minority/gender-relevant policy performance[45]), and the economy's recent and projected performance. The profile provides the facts and conditions used during mission analysis, and a baseline level of knowledge to share understanding with other USG Departments. A foundational requirement exists to support collaboration in order to ensure a common understanding of the operational environment by all participating military and civilian planners.

(2) **Develop a country economic narrative**, based on the data collected in step one, that explains the country's current and prospective economic situation, including identifying the interests of significant economic actors, and the relationship of the dominant drivers of the economy to its overall performance. This narrative provides additional facts for mission analysis and includes assumptions. It should identify:

(a) Pre-conflict problems

(b) How the conflict has affected, and will likely affect, economic performance, especially in key sub-sectors.

(c) How the anticipated post-conflict security environment will affect economic performance.

(d) Ongoing or planned post-conflict reconstruction and stabilization (R&S) programs by the host nation, USG, international and other donor organizations.

(e) Host country willingness and capacity to implement economic recovery programs.

(3) **Identify and analyze the economic drivers of the conflict** so actions can be planned to mitigate the drivers and reduce the risk of a return to conflict. This analysis identifies the economic centers of gravity and critical factors for mission analysis, and initiates development of potential courses of action. This identification and analysis should provide answers to the questions:

(a) What were the economic drivers of the conflict? Ideally this information would be available from the completed collaborative Interagency Conflict Assessment.

(b) How have the drivers affected and been affected by the conflict's outcome?

(c) What are the economic interests of conflict stakeholders and power brokers; and how have those interests influenced the course of the conflict? How has the outcome of the conflict re-arranged the interests of these groups?

(d) What potential measures and courses of action can be taken to reduce these economic influences so that the conflict will not reignite?

(4) **Prepare an economic section for inclusion in an initial staff estimate.** This provides a description of the situation, a mission statement, and outlines potential general courses of action for military support to economic stabilization. Include:

(a) Summary of the structure and performance of the economy, environment, country's economic strategy, and the anticipated post-conflict economic conditions and problems;

(b) USG policy goals; both multilateral and bilateral, if available;

(c) Desired end-state of USG (and other countries involved); and

(d) Potential general courses of action.

The details of conducting an economic assessment are discussed below.

2. Conducting an Economic Assessment

This guide can prepare a JFC to participate with the JS and OSD in an Interagency Conflict Assessment, or to prepare a post-conflict assessment independently. This should establish a baseline condition.

a. **Step One: Compile a Country Economic Profile**. The country economic profile includes quantitative indicators of the performance of the economy as seen in the context of the country's economic strategy and its environment. While such a profile is not sufficient for detailed planning to address problems in specific sub-sectors of the economy, assembling the information will provide insight into the economic system and implications for post-conflict reconstruction and stabilization. The data will be evaluated and coupled with analysis in subsequent steps. A list of the basic data that should be covered in the economic profile is summarized in Table A-1 below. It is useful to start with a single-page summary to better understand the macro environment. A more complete list is contained in Annex B, and an example of a completed profile is in Annex C.

(1) **Economic Indicators of Performance**. There are many sources of data for the economic profile. The recommended profile is based on the State Department Economic Engagement Matrix,[46] Annex A, maintained by the State Department's Bureau of Energy, Economic, and Business Affairs. The matrix in Appendix D provides a snapshot of the most recently available economic information for a single or broad group of countries, with some 90 economic indicators and diplomatic tools. Examples of available diplomatic tools include bilateral or multilateral trade agreements, investment treaties, foreign assistance packages, trade sanctions, and/or debt forgiveness. The economic data come from a number of standardized international databases, including those of the International Monetary Fund (IMF), the World Bank, and regional development banks such as the Asian Development Bank, African Development Bank, Inter-American Development Bank, etc. In addition, various UN agencies (e.g., UNDP and UNICEF) have extensive social databases. The use of diplomatic tools is normally coordinated through the interagency consultation process as well as discussions within the U.N. and other multilateral organizations. Those engagements and tools listed are vetted with appropriate USG offices. Of the many available sources, the Department of State matrix is recommended because it stimulates interaction with the offices in State, USAID, and other departments and agencies with whom the JS, OSD and joint force will develop a plan. The matrix is also useful because of the supporting footnotes, links to data, and ability to compare countries easily. Other off-the-shelf sources to supplement the basic economic data and provide additional analysis include:

(a) *The Economist* magazine's Economist Intelligence Unit (EIU).[47]

(b) World Development Indicators (WDI).[48]

(c) The U.S. Library of Congress Country Study series.[49]

Performance	Environment	Policies
GDP, Rate and Per capita	Demography	Foreign
Prices and Inflation	Natural resources	Defense
Balance of Payments	Geography	Monetary
Employment	Climate	Fiscal
IDPs, Refugees, Ex-Combatants	Institutions	Trade
Official Development Assistance	Corruption	Investment
Poverty rates	Infrastructure	Industrial
Informal Economy	"Doing Business" profile (World Bank)	Social & Educational
		IMF Arrangements (if any)
		Gender

Table A-1. Economic Profile Data

(d) World Bank Country Data at-a-glance profile.[50]

(2) **Assembling and Examining Economic Data to Understand Both the Structure of the Economy and How It Has Performed**. Using the Department of State Economic Engagement Matrix (Annex A) as a baseline, some illustrative questions to assist in understanding the implications of the data include:

(a) Economic and sub-sector indicators discussing internal economic performance:

1. How wealthy is the country (Gross Domestic Product (GDP)), is it growing (GDP growth) and is the value of output per person (GDP per capita) growing? Growth in GDP and GDP per capita are considered broad measures of economic growth.

2. How is the country performing relative to its neighbors, regionally and globally?

3. Is there a functioning and stable currency?

4. What is the rate and trend of inflation?

5. What is the assessed level of government intervention in the market (include major subsidy programs, and price controls and ceilings)?

6. Do Development Indicators such as the GINI Coefficient (a measure of Income Inequality) or the WDI Percentage of Population Living on Less than $1.25/day and Poverty Headcount indicate unequal wealth distribution in the population and severe poverty?

7. What is the structure and basis of the economy? What sub-sectors and industries drive output/GDP? Is it agriculture-based, industrial, dependent on commodities, mining, etc.? Does the country spend an excessive amount on defense or import or export large amounts of arms? Do economic policies favor or discriminate against individual sub-sectors? The best source of this type of information is a Defense Intelligence Agency (DIA) Defense Economic Assessment.

8. How large is the informal economy? AMEMB reporting or academic studies are good sources for this type of information.

(b) Employment data:

1. What is the size of labor force, employment by sub-sector, unemployment rate? Source is World Development Indicators[51] or a recent IMF Article IV report. Estimates of the under employed and partially employed may be used to get a sense of the economically active population.

2. If relevant, number of internally displaced persons (IDPs).[52] This data is difficult to obtain, and may have to be stated as an assumption. Recommend close

coordination with the AMEMB country team and the Joint Staff, OSD, and Department of State (Office of Population, Refugees and Migration).

    3. Number of refugees who have left country. This group is indicative of both possible returnees who may require employment, and also offer key skills and financial resources to the rebuilding effort.

    4. Number of ex-combatants.

    5. Percentage of GDP accounted for by State Owned Enterprises (SOEs).

    6. The level of education within the workforce. Are there operating basic and vocational educational institutions? Linking this to item 3, refugees, may determine the size and extent of the "brain drain" facing the country.

    (c) Trade and investment indicators discuss external performance:

    1. How important is trade to the economy (the percentage of exports/imports to GDP provides the best indication)? What does it indicate in terms of the country's ability to compete in external trading markets?

    2. What is the main composition of trade in goods and services and who are the main trading partners? Are any exports/imports important to the US (EIU)?

    3. How are the country's tariff levels, non-tariff trade barriers, and administration of customs duties affecting trade? Both the Millennium Challenge Corporation (MCC) and "Trade Freedom" from Heritage Foundation Index of Economic Freedom are good sources.

    4. What are the main factors and trends in the current account balance; and how are any deficits being financed? Is deterioration of the current account balance threatening the stability of the currency? For example, a persistent negative current account deficit is indicative of instability; and a possible cause is a trade imbalance that is partially offset by remittances.

    5. To what extent does the country rely on remittances? How are remittances transmitted and what currencies are used? This was added to the State Department list because of its importance in developing countries. Sources are the World Bank and UN International Fund for Agriculture Development.[53]

    6. What is the level and role of Foreign Direct Investment (FDI) in the economy? How are government tax and other policies influencing FDI? Both trade levels and FDI flows provide an indication of how open an economy is to outside investment (EIU)?

    (d) Financial indicators (government budget):

1. Is the country's budget in fiscal balance (Central government receipts minus outlays); and does its trend indicate fiscal stability and good fiscal governance? How large is the deficit as a percentage of GDP?

2. What are the primary sources of revenue and major expenditures? What is the proportion of government revenue to GDP?

3. Is the government implementing fiscal policy recommendations of the IMF, especially to combat inflation and meet critical social needs (defense budget vs. social sector budget)?[54]

4. How does the banking system operate in the country? How many banks are state owned, private and international? What are the general lending practices for businesses, consumers, or to the government to finance public debt? Is the banking system playing a normal intermediary role between savers and lenders, and providing accurate signals to capital markets of costs of borrowing funds?

5. What is the level of banking penetration in the country? Do banks use automated teller machines (ATMs) and telephone/cellular phone banking? Are informal money changers prevalent?

6. Is the country a member of the Financial Action Task Force (FATF) or regional equivalent? Is it a FATF country of primary concern and is money laundering a major concern?

(e) Telecommunications. Cellular penetration has been referred to by some as the revolution of the developing world because of the ability to transfer money. Are cellular telephones a significant means of transferring money?

(f) Economic engagement provides a general indication of the level of formal economic actions and treaties with US and other international organizations.

1. Is the country a member of a regional preferential trade group?

2. Are there any trade disputes or sanctions in force?

(g) Development aid indicators discuss the level of involvement of both US and world development aid.

1. How dependent is the country on development aid? The Organization for Economic Cooperation and Development (OECD) provides data on aid donors and recipients.[55]

2. What is the level of USG engagement? How much funding is being executed by USAID, State Department Economic Support Funds, USAID Trade Capacity Building (TCB), U.S. Trade development Agency (TDA), US Export-Import Bank (EXIM) and others?

(h) Millennium Challenge Corporation (MCC) indicators. Do the MCC indicators show progress toward the goals of ruling justly, investing in people, encouraging economic freedom, and managing toward a sustainable environment? Are good policies being implemented and is country ownership being sustained?

(3) **Environment and Context**. An understanding of the environment and context provides an understanding of the human and natural resources, infrastructure, and institutions that shape the enabling environment. The major sources are the same as in step one, primarily the EIU, Janes, Library of Congress and others as indicated.

(a) **Demography and Geography**

1. What are the population, major population centers, and level of urbanization? How do population age, race, sex ratio, literacy, ethnicity, languages, religions, tribes, or group distribution affect the economy? Understand the concentration or dispersion of major ethnic, linguistic, tribal, or religious groups. Are key political and economic interests divided along urban and rural divisions and interests? Source is Janes Sentinel Security Assessments.[56]

2. What are the population dynamics from the World Development Indicators,[57] US Census Bureau International Database, Gridded Population of the World and the Global Rural-Urban Mapping Project (GRUMP),[58] and World Health Organization Statistics Report?[59] This includes total population, population by sex, population by age group, population growth rate, crude birth rate, crude death rate, age dependency ratio, fertility rate, life expectancy, infant and under-five mortality rate (disaggregate by sex), adult mortality rate, and probability of survival to age 65.[60]

3. What are the major geographic features (arable land, mountains, and harbors) and who controls them? What are the country's policies for tenure and land control issues?

4. What are the country's natural resources, who controls them, and what impact does their exploitation have on the environment?

5. Does the country have economically and militarily strong neighbors, proximity to developed trading partners and export markets?

6. Does the country border on states with civil or ethnic conflict or insurgency? Are insurgent groups from the target country carrying out operations from camps or bases in a neighboring country?

7. What is the distribution of income by demographic groups such as regions, age, religion, ethnic groups, tribes, etc?

8. Does the educational system develop human capital that can sustain and grow the economy, from early childhood development through vocational and higher education?

(b) **Domestic Political and Institutional Context.** In addition to the information on historical context, regime type, legitimacy and related subjects normally available in the intelligence estimate:

<u>1</u>. What is the role of the government in the economy?

<u>2</u>. What percentage of GDP does the government control?

<u>3.</u> What are the government institutions that regulate and provide a competitive environment? Do cartels, banks, or other mechanisms limit competition?

<u>4.</u> Is there an independent and impartial judiciary in commercial matters? Are contracts effectively enforced?

<u>5.</u> Does the law provide for an independent Central Bank and is it effective and independent in practice?

<u>6.</u> How strong are business institutions such as banks, infrastructure, agriculture, labor? Is economic power centralized in the hands of a few? What are the key business institutions and how effective are they in influencing government policy? Are there business and trade associations (e.g., chambers of commerce) that are active and effectively represent their membership's interests)?

<u>7.</u> What is the role of trade unions in the country?

<u>8</u>. How did economic infrastructure contribute to or detract from the country's competiveness? Good sources are EIU and the Global Competitiveness Report.[61]

<u>9.</u> Is there an effective civil service? What is the general quality of public officials? Do they competently and honestly manage government institutions?

(c) **Security Context**

<u>1</u>. How does the security sector (police, military, and judiciary) affect the economic environment?

<u>2</u>. To what degree is the security sector involved in illegal economic activity?

<u>3</u>. What is the military's role in the economy?

(4) **Strategy, Goals, and Policies**. This section should state existing policies and the current economic views of the host government and USG and other international actors economic views toward the host government if known. The US rarely undertakes stability operations alone; and the international community has a well articulated approach to stability operations. For example, the UNDP, World Bank and IMF are usually tasked with conducting an initial post-conflict needs assessment and coordinate short-term

priorities with the host nation. This usually becomes the basis for the engagement of international agencies and frequently becomes the basis for the host country's own strategy. While various stakeholders can be expected to have differing views regarding the pace of stabilization, priorities, and who should pay for assistance, the USG and key international economic organizations will agree on most of the broad objectives of post-conflict reconstruction and stabilization assistance. The joint force should be aware of the economic strategy and policies established by the host government and any changes recommended by the USG in concert with the IMF and World Bank. These will help identify constraints and restraints during the mission analysis and, although they apply primarily to the macro national government level, the policies influence and affect actions at the local level where joint forces will operate. The joint plan should strive to align with and support the host nation strategy. The JS and OSD participate actively with the Departments of Treasury and State, which represent the US in these processes, and should provide joint force planners the host nation and International Financial Institutions (IFI) plans. The policies of specific interest to understand are:

(a) **Fiscal Policy**

<u>1</u>. What is the government revenue target from all sources?

<u>2</u>. What is the government expenditure target and priorities, such as security services, military, social, etc.?

<u>3</u>. What is the projected deficit; and how does the government propose to pay/offset it?

<u>4</u>. What are the USG, IMF, and World Bank views on the fiscal policy?

(b) **Trade Policy**

<u>1</u>. What are the tariff, nontariff incentives, and barriers to trade?

<u>2</u>. What is the border management policy? Does it interfere with trade?

(c) **Industrial Policy**

<u>1</u>. Do state-owned enterprises exist; and does the government policy privatize or maintain state-owned enterprises?

<u>2</u>. Does the government subsidize or provide directed loans to State-Owned Enterprises (SOEs)?

<u>3</u>. Do taxes and selective policies favor one industry over others?

<u>4</u>. Is there a labor policy that unnecessarily restricts employers from hiring or dismissing employees? Does the government protect the right of workers to organize independent trade unions?

(e) **Education and Social Policies**

<u>1</u>. What are the social safety net and poverty reduction/welfare policies?

<u>2</u>. What are the public health and education policies?

<u>3</u>. Are there policies on religion, immigration, or cultural areas?

b. **Step Two: Developing a Country Economic Narrative – Evaluate the Data**. The second step for planners in the assessment process is to develop an economic analysis and narrative that relates the broad economic, political and social trends present in the country to one another and to national and international trends. The State Department's Economic Engagement Matrix referenced above supports the comparison of a country within a region and with its neighbors. The assessment analyzes the data collected in step one to identify the post-conflict problems in the economy, describes how the conflict has or is likely to affect the course of the economy, and supports identification and prioritization of Joint Force economic stabilization support tasks. While the questions that should be addressed in the economic narrative will vary with HN conditions and level of development, the economic narrative should focus on identifying specific problem areas that could be addressed by joint forces. Sources of material for an economic narrative include:

(1) **Situation Analysis and Policy Formulation**. If the Department of State is leading whole-of-government planning, identifying major mission elements (strategic objectives) to address major problems will have been completed during the situation analysis overview and policy formulation.

(2) The Department of Treasury can provide USG economic objectives and priorities. Treasury can additionally explain multilateral agreements such as:

(a) IMF *Stand-By Arrangement*, that is frequently the key framework for economic reform and contain performance criteria.

(b) IMF *Article IV Consultation Reports* that contain detailed data on fiscal and monetary policies, identifies issues facing the country, and offers policy prescriptions.

(c) IMF *Staff Reports* that address whether governments are meeting targets established in formal strategy papers, called *Letters of Intent* and specify elements of a country's recovery plan. Successfully meeting these targets is a pre-condition for IMF loans.[62]

(d) Analyses from the World Bank, the UN Development Program (UNDP), UN Food and Agriculture Organization, and other multilateral organizations.

(3) Commercially published analyses from *The Economist's* EIU, Janes, and others.

(4) Economic reporting by US embassies, analysis by intelligence agencies, and information and analysis gathered through direct contact with AMEMB officers and USG agencies.[63]

(5) USAID produces analytical reports that provide a summary of the economic growth performance in countries that receive USAID support. The point of contact regarding these country reports is the Economic Growth Office of USAID's Bureau of Economic Growth, Agriculture and Trade (EGAT).

(6) Various domestic and international press reports and publications.

The table below provides illustrative questions contained in an economic narrative.

c. **Step Three: Analyze the Economic Drivers of the Conflict**. The third step in the assessment process is to identify and understand the economic drivers of the conflict.

ILLUSTRATIVE QUESTIONS FOR THE ECONOMIC NARRATIVE
(identifying trends and comparisons, which should be considered in the local context)

OBJECTIVES
What are HN and USG objectives for R&S?
Are International Organizations (World Bank, IMF and others) engaged and do their objectives align with USG objectives?
Is there host nation capacity and political will to conduct economic stabilization?

HOW DID THE CONFLICT AFFECT
Commercial infrastructure, including roads, ports, airports, pipelines, communication facilities, power generation and distribution networks?
Availability of banking services and credit?
Manufacturing capacity?
Agricultural sub-sector?
Educational sub-sector?

STRENGTHS AND WEAKNESSES
Based on the data in the profile, what are the strengths and weaknesses in the economy?
Does the level of funding support the security sector strategy and assigned missions in defense, police, border management, etc?
What are the centers of economic power and what role are they taking?
How does corruption affect the government administration of the economy?
In what areas is productivity growing or declining?
What is blocking economic growth?
Does the rule of law and judicial capacity enable private property and contract enforcement?
Does the macroeconomic environment and policy create high inflation and discourage risk?
Is there competition?
Where does the economic performance not match the policy/strategy (e.g., policy of fiscal discipline but increasing inflation.)?
Does the physical infrastructure adequately support the economy?
Is investment constrained by lack of property rights, human resources or monetary capital?

SECURITY
Is there a secure environment for citizens and businesses to conduct their day-to-day activities? Describe any restrictions on the free movement of persons or goods and address international trade.
Is the government able to protect key assets, such as official buildings, property records, and critical infrastructure?
Does the security environment enable donor agencies and organizations to conduct their day-to-day activities?
Does displacement (Internally Displaced Persons (IDPs)) cause significant humanitarian or security problems in the country or in neighboring countries?
Are significant numbers of people leaving the country through fear?
If there has been a demobilization of the armed forces, how is this affecting security, stability and the work force?

Table A-2. Illustrative Questions for the Economic Narrative

Drivers of conflict include the dynamics resulting from key actors' mobilization of social groups around core grievances. Core grievances can be understood as the potential energy of conflict.[64] Potential courses of action should reduce these drivers and increase institutional capacity to handle them, thereby minimizing the risk of a return to conflict. As noted by USAID, promoting economic growth in a post-conflict environment means doing things differently from the way economic development is ordinarily handled in stable developing countries:

> *"Post-conflict economic growth programs must address as directly as possible the factors that led to the conflict, taking into account the fragility of the environment. Planning has to be based on much more than narrow technical consideration of economic efficiency and growth stimulation. Programs also must be effective at opening up opportunities and increasing inclusiveness; they should be judged in part on the basis of whether or not they help mitigate political factors that increase the risk or a return to hostilities."[65]*

(1) Economic grievances and conflict drivers may include socioeconomic differences, frequently aggravated by low incomes or slow economic growth, unequal distribution of societal benefits or burdens, and marginalization of vulnerable groups or geographic regions. Other drivers include competition for natural resources, (e.g., water and arable land), or for easily tradable natural resources, such as diamonds, energy commodities, and metals.

(2) A comprehensive *Interagency Conflict Assessment* should be conducted which identifies the drivers of conflict. If unavailable, recommend conducting a *Conflict Assessment* with USAID, or using the USAID *Conflict Assessment Framework*.[66] USAID and each Geographic Combatant Command have assigned liaison officers who can coordinate this with the JS, OSD, and USAID.

(3) Another software tool is the Measuring Progress in Conflict Environments (MPICE)[67] framework, which proposes common drivers of conflict such as illicit wealth and corruption, economic inequality, weak institutions, external influences and others which can be tailored to the context. MPICE additionally proposes objectives and an extensive list of generic metrics which can be tailored to the specific application and used to measure progress.

d. **Step 4: Draft an Economic Estimate**. The final step in the assessment process is to distill material that has been assembled in the first three steps into a staff estimate. That provides a basis to develop potential courses of action to promote rebuilding of the economy, reduce economic drivers of the conflict, and build HN institutional capacity. It should include these components:

(1) A summary of the post-conflict economic situation and where it is trending based on the country's economic profile and current condition. This should include a discussion of the economic interests of individual stakeholders and groups as well as short term and long term economic threats and opportunities to prioritize intervention efforts.

(2) A list of the main economic problems anticipated in the post-conflict period both immediately and beyond the period of initial stabilization, the impact of those problems

on the course of the conflict, and the political will of the host government to address them. Problems related to security, governance and rule of law that, if not corrected, that can impede or block economic rebuilding over the medium term should be included.

(3) A list of the actions that the host government, international organizations, and foreign donors are expected to take to address those problems listed above over defined set of timeframes that are congruent with the actions.

(4) A summary of the main conclusions of the analysis of the economic drivers of the conflict.

(5) Potential general courses of action based on level of effort and sequencing of USG strategic objectives. As illustrated below, the levels of effort assigned to potential tasks form the basis of general course of action matrix and are related directly to the security situation. Table A-3 below, provides a snap-shot of potential general courses of action based on level of effort and the security environment during a post-conflict assessment. The probability data reflects the immediate post-conflict period.

Security Environment	Hostile	Hostile	Uncertain	Uncertain	Uncertain
Government Services	None	Basic	Basic	Expanding	Restored
Potential Military Tasks	Probability of Requirement				
Providing Security	High	High	High	High	High
Protecting Gov't Records/Assets	High	High	Medium	Medium	Medium
Protecting Critical Infrastructure	High	High	Medium	Medium	Medium
Generating Employment	Medium	High	High	High	Medium
Restoring Damaged Infrastructure	Medium	High	Medium	Medium	Low
Supporting Private sector Development	Low	Medium	Medium	Low	Low
Supporting Ag. Development	Low	Medium	Medium	Low	Low
Supporting Gov't Capacity Building	Low	Medium	Low	Low	Low
Supporting Economic Reforms	Low	Low	Low	Low	Low

Table A-3. Probability of Military Tasks

SECTION B. HOW TO CONDUCT AN EMPLOYMENT GENERATION ASSESSMENT

3. Employment Sub-sector Overview

These questions should go beyond those in the comprehensive assessment, Section A, and be designed to reveal detail about the sub-sector that will enable designers and planners to identify possible courses of action. Examples include:

a. What is the impact of the current security situation on employment and economic activity? In what ways did the conflict affect productive economic activity by those employed in both the formal and informal economy?

b. What is the working-age population of the country? How is it distributed? Where are the major population centers?

c. How large is the work force in each area?

d. What are the expectations of the population with regard to employment in the post-conflict era?

e. Is the economy mostly agrarian, or industrial, manufacturing-based, or mixed? What are the key industries and companies? Where are major manufacturing facilities located?

f. How dependent on foreign trade is local industry, either for key components or for export markets?

g. Do the economy's existing labor regulations pose barriers to employment?

h. How difficult is it to hire or fire workers? What are the costs of firing a worker?

i. Are there restrictions on when and how long employees can work?

j. What percentage of salary are non-wage labor costs such as social security payments and payroll taxes?

4. Institutional Capacity and Resource Availability

These questions should identify organizational, financial, and human resources available for: 1) meeting critical short-term problems, and 2) addressing longer-term gaps that require governmental/institutional capacity building. They should also identify Host Nation, USG, other foreign donor government, intergovernmental organization, and NGOs operating in the area or that may offer resources to support employment generation activities. Examples include:

a. What are the major government ministries and departments with employment generation or vocational training responsibilities? Are there any government or private sector vocational training facilities? Do they have the administrative and financial capabilities to implement employment generation programs? How can their efforts be supported?

b. Which ministry or organization is responsible for enforcing domestic labor laws and regulations? Do workers have the right to organize independent unions?

c. What are the important labor organizations/unions? What roles are they likely to play in employment generation? Supportive? Confrontational? Do they have links to specific groups?

d. What kinds of potential funding and technical assistance may be available from the USG?

e. Were other foreign governments or international development institutions active in the country pre-crisis? What type of programs were they funding? Could they be restarted quickly? How might they be supported?

f. Were foreign or domestic NGOs active in the country prior to the crisis? What type of employment generation programs were they funding? Is there a potential for these to be restarted quickly?

g. Are there any existing donor coordination groups active in the country? How are they organized? Where do they meet?

5. Problem Identification and Analysis

Questions should be designed to identify problems in the sub-sector as well as their scope and causes. It should help planners identify problems that the JTF, civilian USG agencies, and coalition partners could address directly and the needs for long-term capacity building that would be initiated by the military and completed by civilian agencies or be conducted entirely by civilian agencies. Examples include:

a. How do government actions and policies affect employment generation? Does the government impose undue restrictions on labor mobility (wage controls, restrictions on hiring and firing, wage taxes, etc.)? Are there unnecessary levels of bureaucracy?

b. Which components of the labor force are most sensitive to unemployment in the sense that their failure to meet their economic aspirations in the post-conflict era could undermine the achievement of mission objectives?

c. How has it been affected by demobilized soldiers? How many combatants are being demobilized? What are their employment prospects? How high is the risk they will become insurgents or turn to criminal activity if their employment expectations are not met?

d. How has employment been affected by IDPs? How many internally displaced persons (IDPs) have left their homes and where are they located? How many people have fled the country as refugees and where are they located now?

e. Has there been a loss of skills in the private sector and government due to crisis? Are there programs in place to identify members of these groups and encourage their return?

f. Are there specific laws or regulations that hinder employment generation efforts? How might these be addressed?

6. Potential for Unintended Consequences

Questions would seek to identify the potential that operations in the sub-sector might strengthen spoilers or disturb societal fault lines/divisions between ethnic or religious groups, social classes, or tribes/clans. Examples include:

a. Were there issues in the employment sub-sector that contributed to the conflict or crisis? These may include wide spread unemployment, ethnic or social tensions.

b. Were there groups that benefited most from the pre-conflict status quo? How might they respond to possible courses of action?

c. How high is the risk that public support will shift away from the leadership supported by the United States if popular expectations regarding employment are not met?

d. Are some ethnic, religious, or other groups more affected than others? Are there particular groups whose needs require special attention, or pose risk of creating tensions? Examples include potential for a rapid influx of demobilizing combatants who will be competing for employment with women who, as a group, increased their presence in the job market during the conflict, as the number of women-headed households increased.

e. How have SOEs been affected? Are employees still drawing wages? Who controls these entities? Who would benefit from resumption in operation specific SOEs?

f. Are there high levels of informal economic activity? How do these compare to pre-crisis levels? Are any of these informal activities supported or controlled by criminal or potential spoiler groups?

SECTION C. ESSENTIAL ELEMENTS OF AN AGRICULTURAL SUB-SECTOR ASSESSMENT

7. Agriculture Sub-Sector Assessment Outline: Key Questions for Joint Planners

a. **Sub-Sector-Specific Overview**. These questions should go beyond those in the comprehensive assessment, Section A, and be designed to reveal detail about the sub-sector that will enable planners to identify possible courses of action. Examples include:

(1) What is the agricultural component of gross domestic product (GDP), and projections for the future? What role does agriculture play in the local and overall economy? Is this role growing or declining? Why? What are the key factors affecting production? What are potential areas of comparative advantage requiring further investment and technical assistance? What is the likely growth trend for the sub-sector? What is the extent of import dependence for national food requirements? And what is potential for domestic agriculture to substitute for import demand?

(2) How large is overall labor force in the agriculture sub-sector, including processing and marketing activities? What percentage grows crops, raises livestock, or depends on post-harvest activities for income? Are there regional difference in income and production?

(3) What are the landholding patterns—large scale commercial, smallholders, tenant farmers, cash crop cultivation versus subsistence farming? What is the average sized land holding? What measurements are used to define them (e.g., acres, hectares, biggahs, etc)? Is land reform a potential issue? Is mechanized farming prevalent or are draught animals still widely used? An analysis of the impact each major crop has on employment would also be useful.

(4) What are the historical production profiles for domestic food and cash crops? This should provide a historical record of each major crop produced. This would include data on recent harvests, how that compares to historical trends, and an assessment of possible reasons for any significant changes in harvest levels or market demand.

(5) What are the key inputs used for crop production (e.g., seed, fertilizer, irrigation, etc.)? Are these inputs distributed by free market mechanisms or government control? Are subsidies involved? What are the import requirements for major inputs?

(6) What are the key transaction costs faced by producers? What factors add to the cost of production? Are there government levies or taxes that affect production? Are these broad based or targeted at specific crops? Are power or irrigation costs unnecessarily high due to inefficiencies or specific government policies? What inefficiencies exist in value chains that keep costs high or make certain crops less competitive relative to imports?

(7) Does food security exist, as defined by all people having access to sufficient, safe, nutritious food? The concept of food security is defined as including both physical and economic access (sufficient income) to food that meets people's dietary needs, as well as their food preferences. Does the country produce sufficient food to meet basic needs? Is there a system of warehouses and stockpiles to meet unexpected shortages? Are there regional imbalances? Are there programs in place to identify and assist vulnerable groups?

(8) How do farmers finance production? Is there a crop finance system in place? Does it differ from crop to crop? Are there any cooperative or microfinance activities?

(9) How important is commercial agriculture (i.e., cultivation of cash crops) in the economy? What are the main crops produced for export? How have these crops performed? Are there unique factors (e.g., taxes, export constraints, price controls) affecting their performance?

(10) What are the major domestic and international corporations and businesses producing, processing, or marketing in agriculture? Major producers of agricultural inputs (e.g., seeds, fertilizer, and machinery) should be included.

(11) What is the role and effectiveness of producer organizations? What are the existing local producer organizations (e.g., cooperative societies, farmers' associations, etc.)? Can these local organizations serve as effective partners; and will they support joint force recovery efforts? Are these organizations locally controlled? How are they viewed by the local population?

(12) What is the role of agriculture in government's general economic development strategy? How does it fit into any existing national development strategies and targets?

(13) How does the current strategy compare to the pre-crisis agricultural sub-sector development strategy and program? Such strategies may have been formally adopted by the government, or contained in proposals by the World Bank, or other donors.

b. **Institutional Capacity and Resource Availability**. Questions should identify organizational, financial, and human resources available for: 1) meeting critical short-term problems, and 2) addressing longer-term gaps that require governmental/institutional capacity building. These should also identify Host Nation, USG, other foreign donor government, intergovernmental organization, and NGOs operating in the area or that may offer resources to support employment generation activities. Examples include:

(1) What are the major government ministries and departments with responsibilities affecting the agriculture sub-sector, including food safety and health issues? Are there any government sponsored research facilities? How are agribusinesses regulated?

(2) How is government organized at the local level, especially in rural areas? Do local entities have taxing authority?

(3) Is there an agriculture extension service or similar assistance to farmers that provides improved farming techniques and production efficiencies through communication and education? How well do these entities perform?

(4) Is there capacity for doing research and performing on-farm trials of new seed varieties or different production strategies by crop?

(5) What kinds of potential funding and technical assistance are available from the USG?

(6) Were other foreign governments or international development institutions active in the country prior to the crisis? What type of programs were they funding? Is there a potential for these to be restarted quickly?

(7) Were foreign or domestic NGOs active in the country prior to the crisis? What type of programs were they funding? Is there a potential for these to be restarted quickly?

(8) Are there any existing donor coordination groups active in the country? How are they organized? Where do they meet?

c. **Problem Identification and Analysis.** Questions should be designed to identify problems in the sub-sector as well as their scope and causes. They should help planners to identify: 1) problems that the JTF, civilian USG agencies, and coalition partners could address directly, and 2) needs for long-term capacity building that would be initiated by the military and completed by civilian agencies, or be conducted entirely by civilian agencies. Examples include:

(1) How has the crisis affected activity in the agriculture sub-sector? Has there been damage to irrigation systems, warehouses or other key infrastructure? Does the general security situation prevent cultivation or delivery of agricultural production to market? Have sowing or harvesting activities been affected? Are there potential projects that may limit damage to crops in the field or to food stockpiles?

(2) Are there environmental issues that may affect agricultural production? Does soil degradation, desertification, deforestation, declining water resources, or similar things restrict production? Can any of these be addressed by changes in current practices?

(3) What is limiting agricultural production? Could production be increased by better inputs of seeds, modern tools, or improved irrigation? Are there weaknesses in the transport and communications infrastructure? Do growers have access to current market information? Are prices set by the government or the free market natural forces?

(4) How do government actions and policies affect the agricultural sub-sector? Does the government impose price controls, subsidies, taxation or other distortions that negatively affect the agricultural income or production levels? Countries sometimes subsidize food as a component of a social safety net to protect the poor. In the US, the Food Stamp and School Breakfast and Lunch programs are examples. Export bans that prevent farmers from benefiting from high world food prices are another example. Are there unnecessary levels of bureaucracy?

(5) Are there any unique factors that affect agriculture or food security? One example of this may be the impact of HIV on the agricultural sub-sector in sub-Saharan Africa, but other issues could include long term drought conditions, or locust attacks that affected the Sahel region of Africa in the late 1980's and early 2000's.

d. **Potential for Unintended Consequences.** Questions would seek to identify the potential that operations in the sub-sector might strengthen spoilers or disturb societal fault lines/divisions between ethnic or religious groups, social classes, or tribes/clans. Examples include:

(1) Were there issues in the agriculture sub-sector that contributed to the conflict or crisis? These may include land tenure issues, water or grazing rights, ethnic tensions or similar issues.

(2) What were the groups that benefited most from the pre-conflict status quo? How might they respond to proposed courses of action?

e. The assessment of the agriculture sub-sector should include a description of how the local population responds to possible incentives and disincentives. Intelligence analysts with regional expertise can be helpful in predicting how the local population may respond to new incentive structures. A simplistic example is one that seeks to discourage farmers from growing opium or coca and transition to growing legal "alternative crops" that yield much lower returns. While government officials may understand the financial advantages of growing the elicit crop, they may not fully understand that there are other factors impacting on local growers - the threat of harm from the drug traffickers and possible resentment from "arbitrary" crop eradication methods. The result from an incomplete understanding of the local incentive structure may therefore not only fail to convince farmers to grow alternative crops; but eradication efforts may motivate farmers to seek help from the drug traffickers or join destabilizing activities.

SECTION D. ESSENTIAL ELEMENTS OF A FINANCIAL SUB-SECTOR ASSESSMENT

8. Key Assessment Information

The comprehensive assessment from Section A is generally all that is required. However, ensure that assessments from DOT, DOS, IMF, and the World Bank are available and there is an understanding of (1) The previous and ongoing IMF, World Bank, and regional development bank programs that support reconstituting the financial sub-sector; (2) Programs by foreign donor countries and NGOs attempting to reconstitute the country financial sub-sector, restore commercial banking activity, and expand the availability of credit to business; and (3) The availability of business credit to small and medium enterprises.

9. Identification Requirements

a. National and sub-national government entities that cannot purchase goods and services, pay salaries, or engage in other public financial sub-sector operations due to hostile or uncertain conditions.

b. Areas and regions where commercial credit to small and medium enterprises is not available because banks and other lenders cannot operate due to hostile or uncertain conditions.

APPENDIX B
S/CRS POST-CONFLICT RECONSTRUCTION ESSENTIAL TASKS

Goal: Respond to Immediate Needs and Establish Foundation for Development

1. Economic Stabilization - Employment Generation

	Task	USG D/A	IGO	NGO	Private Sector	Specify Agent(s) /Remarks
DOD Funding	Request flexible and immediate funding for work initiatives and grants Contingency Contracting Funding	DOD				Request flexible and immediate Contingency Contract Funding (similar to Afghan & Iraq CERP)
Freedom of Movement (From SECURITY)	Ensure freedom of movement	DOD				The essential ingredient
	Dismantle roadblocks and establish checkpoints	DOD				See TRADE - Review tariffs, tax structures and impediments to trade
	Regulate air and overland movement	DOD DHS				DHS (CBP & ICE) can provide technical assistance in customs, border control, immigration, etc
Public Works Jobs	Design and implement labor-intensive quick impact initiatives to provide immediate employment, soliciting projects ideas from local communities	DOD, USAID	WB	X	Intl Chamber of Commerce	USAID Country Mission supported by Washington offices DCHA (OFDA/OTI/CMM), EGAT and others Determine if employment or completing the project is more important and use labor intensive methods when possible Facilitate local organization
	Rationalize public works projects with long-term development program	USAID	X	X	X	Use CMOC or similar environment Request USAID assistance (embedded planner if available) in planning for a Community Based approach program
	Establish temporary employment centers	USAID DOL	UNDP	X		Partner with local government or leaders Facilitate the venue and interaction

		USAID, DOL	WFP			
	Create opportunities for young males, including food for work	X		X	X	USAID, Depts. of Labor (ILA/OTLA), Commerce, Agriculture.
	Create opportunities for women and children	X		X		USAID, Dept of Labor (ILA/OTLA)
	Create Sports facilities and environments	X		X		USAID
Reintegration of Combatants (From SECURITY)	Obtain (or request support to design) reintegration strategy, including absorptive capacity of economic and social sectors	USAID	UN will usually lead DDR			Resources and tools available at www.unddr.org
	Coordinate DDR plans with overall political and economic recovery plans	DOD, USAID	UN	X		
	Provide jobs, pensions or other material support for demobilized forces	USAID	UN	X		
	Reintegrate ex-combatants into society	USAID	UN	X		
	Provide job training, health screening, education, and employment assistance for demobilized forces	USAID	UN	X		Ensure vocational options are viable. Provide options other than agriculture, basket weaving, etc. consistent with local conditions. Caution: Seek legal advice on funding for employment of former military or paramilitary forces, as funding can be tied to the forces' history of participation in human rights abuses, terrorism, or other criminal activity.
	Employ ex-combatants alongside others to rebuild community infrastructure.	USAID	UN	X		

Micro and Small Enterprise Stimulation				An implied task of country team coordination or may require surveys as part of Tactical Conflict Assessment
Assess skills deficiencies	USAID			
Assess market opportunities for particular skills	USAID			
Create opportunities for vocational educations	USAID DOL			
Skills Training and Counseling				An implied task of country team coordination or may require surveys as part of Tactical Conflict Assessment
Assess and determine immediately employable labor force for appropriate critical and emergency needs	USAID			
Organize and mobilize local and foreign assistance necessary to initiate training and development of vital skills	USAID			Task to CMOC or similar coordination mechanism

2. Economic Stabilization - Market Economy

	Task	USG D/A	IGO	NGO	Private Sector	Specify Agent(s) /Remarks
Private sector Development (*See Legal & Regulatory Reform, Competition Policy*)	Assess the depth of the private sector, including weakness of the goods and service sector and its distribution channels					
	Identify and remove/mitigate obstacles to private sector development (i.e., barriers to entry, high import taxes, import restrictions, lack of business credit, lack of power, telecommunications or transport, non-repatriation of profits)					Use World Bank "Doing Business" indicators and popular reforms as guide
	Jump start small-scale private sector entrepreneurs through grants and loans to micro-entrepreneurs and small and medium enterprises (SMEs)					
	Encourage investment by international actors, including diasporas communities	USAID DOC OPIC	WB	X	X	OPIC provides support for the creation of privately-owned and managed investment funds which invest in new, expanding or privatizing companies. Treasury/Commerce can facilitate visits that establish banking correspondent relations that would deepen commercial relationships between host nation and international businesses.
	Ensure no unfair or unusual restrictions on entry into (i.e., monopoly) and exit from market (i.e., bankruptcy law)					

Category	Task	Agencies	Notes
	Ensure non-preferential access to markets		
	Strengthen private sector through contracting/out-sourcing		Use host country contractors using local employees
	Assess and make recommendations for improvements in condition of power, transport, and telecommunication sub-sectors		
	Provide investors with legal protections and incentives	USAID DOC	Part of Commercial Law Development Program
	Establish a business environment for long-term growth		Security is the essential ingredient
	Offer risk protection to facilitate sustained investment	OPIC	OPIC provides political risk insurance and supports investment funds.
	Promote business growth through regulatory streamlining and sound tax policy	USAID	
	Facilitate the grown of the real sub-sector through development of business associations, think tanks, etc.	USAID DOC	Facilitate and encourage partnerships of cities, States, Trade Associations, Chambers of Commerce, etc. by providing facilities, logistics, communications, etc
	Develop a business strategy/plan for a diversified economy	Treasury USAID	
Bank Lending (From FINANCIAL)	Provide immediate credit including access to micro and SME lending	USAID WB	

Trade From TRADE	Develop on-going credit programs including access to micro and SME lending	USAID		
	Review tariffs, tax structures and impediments to trade	USAID DOC Treasury	WB	US Trade Representative provides trade policy
Small and Micro-enterprise Regime	Identify constraints to small business development and take steps to remove them where possible in the short-term (i.e., lack of credit, onerous taxes)		WB	Use World Bank "Doing Business" indicators and popular reforms as guide
	Develop strategy for removing obstacles to small business development and implement the strategy			
	Assess need for assistance program for small development programs - (technical and financial)	USAID DOC		
	Support development of business associations	USAID DOC		
	Design and draft legal framework for small business development	USAID DOC		USAID and Commerce Department Commercial Law Development Program.
	Help identify funding sources and implement priority projects	USAID DOC		
	Working with IFC and other institutions, explore option to develop micro-enterprise/micro credit entity	USAID Treasury	WB	

		DOC, USAID, DOD (support)	WB	
Privatization	Assess impact of State Owned Enterprises (SOE) on fiscal balance to determine whether fiscal drain or resource loss from unproductive firms can be offset through some type of privatization			Understand and provide input to USG policy. Lessons learned recommend operating SOEs as a major source of employment, and developing a long term transition plan to privatization.
Natural Resources and Environment	Assess and secure access to valuable natural resources			
	Initiate process for addressing and resolving resource ownership and access issues			
	Conduct national environmental survey			

Intentionally Blank

Military Support To Economic Stabilization

APPENDIX C
EXTENDED ESSENTIAL TASKS

The following matrices expand on the activities identified by the S/CRS Essential Task Matrix. The identification of specific tasks that could potentially contribute to banking and finance should be negotiated with the lead US agency and coordinated with the AMEMB country team. Emphasis should be given to anticipating how short-term efforts can be integrated into the overall USG strategy and longer-term reforms and projects.

STAKEHOLDERS, STRATEGY, AND INFRASTRUCTURE					
	Task	USG	IGO	NGO /Private Sector	Specify Agent(s) /Remarks
Review Strategic Objectives	Review Economic Assessment and Strategic Objectives	State Treas USAID DOD	UN		Include IOs and private sector if possible
Review Existing Programs	Coordinate with the country team to review existing programs from Mission Strategic Plan and USAID Country Assistance Strategy	State Treas USAID DOD	UN		
Private Institutions and Key Leaders	Protect key political and societal leaders	DOD			Include key government and private sector personnel involved in information technology in both government and major commercial banking and finance (Chief Information Officers)
	Protect government economic institutions	DOD			Includes financial institutions
	Protect and secure critical infrastructure, natural resources, civil registries, property ownership documents	DOD			Include government and private information technology systems for banking and finance
Critical Facilities	Secure records, storage, equipment and funds related to banking and finance	DOD			Include government and private information technology systems for banking and finance

MONETARY POLICY

	Task	USG	IGO	NGO /Private Sector	Specify Agent(s) /Remarks
Central Bank Operations	Initiate immediate capacity in Central Bank to conduct essential operations such as: * Make domestic payments and settlements and int'l payments* Issue new currency* Prepare balance sheet* Issue letters of credit * Reconcile and report on Treasury accounts* Stabilize currency through devaluation, reduce volume of money in circulation, etc* Cooperate with IMF, World Bank, other regional and donor central banks* Review/prepare bank licensing regulations; * Strengthen bank prudential and supervisory oversight. (See Banking sector); (Control and supervise commercial banking)	Treasury; FRB; USAID;DOD Support	IMFWorld Bank	Major intl commrcl banks	Assessment of central bank operations and its capacity to implement monetary policy should be available from general economic assessment completed in Appendix A. IMF and World Bank normally lead initial assessments and coordinate short term priorities with the host nation. The country team, State, USAID, Treasury, FRB and State (with other donors) provide additional technical assistance beyond the IMF and World Bank. Joint forces support civilian efforts with security and logistics. Also conduct operations with awareness of civilian plans. Whole of government planning should identify any requirements for DOD providing special expertise, essential equipment (office equipment, computers, etc), physical rehabilitation, refurbish essential facilities, etc…
	* Determine skill capacity of key central bank individuals, and if necessary facilitate return of Diaspora	Treasury FRB USAID	IMF World Bank UN IOM	Multinatl Technlgy Corp	A civilian agency, host nation, private sector function. USG agencies can provide technical assistance. For example – 2006 Hewlett Packard (HP) and UN Educational, Scientific and Cultural Organization (UNESCO) project "Piloting Solutions for Reversing Brain Drain into Brain Gain for Africa"
Monetary Audit	Conduct central bank audit	Treasury FRB USAID	IMF World Bank		Longer term civilian action

Macro-Policy and Exchange Rates (See Fiscal Policy and Governance)	Develop/implement basic monetary policy and stabilize prices and manage inflation (i.e., set up currency auction)	Treasury FRB USAID	IMF World Bank	Capability assessment and priorities should be available from general economic assessment in Chap 1 Civilian agency function
	Develop credible exchange rate policy, review currency status and take needed steps to ensure credibility (i.e., prepare for new currency if needed)	Treasury FRB	IMF World Bank	Longer term civilian action
	Introduce national currency if needed	Treasury FRB DOD Support	IMF World Bank	DOD support with security, logistics, distribution, etc
	Develop policy instruments to manage monetary policy consistent with macro-economic programs (e.g., T-Bills, currency auctions)	Treasury	IMFWorld Bank	Longer term civilian action
	Address issues of parallel exchange rates and black market rates if exchange rate distortions exist	Treasury; FRB DOD Support	IMF World Bank	DOD support with information and intelligence sharing
Monetary Statistics	Survey statistical capabilities within the Central Bank and other key Ministries to ensure basic monetary, fiscal, and other economic data are available and collect key statistics	Treasury Commerce FRB USAID		* Longer term civilian action DOC (BEA) can facilitate visits and dialogue with the U.S. Bureau of Census, the Bureau of Labor Statistics, and the Economics and Statistics Administration.

FISCAL POLICY AND GOVERNANCE

	Task	USG	IGO	NGO /Private Sector	Specify Agent(s) /Remarks
Fiscal and Macro-Economic Policy (See Macro Policy and Exchange Rates)	Assess immediate fiscal balance and financing gap and take steps to close fiscal gap	Treasury USAID; DOD	IMF World Bank		Assessment and priorities should be available from general economic assessment completed in Appendix A. Initial action is to start the dialogue to rationalize spending and increase revenue.
Treasury Operations	Reestablish government payment mechanisms to pay recurrent and emergency expenditures	Treasury USAID; DOD			In hostile and uncertain environments, DOD should be prepared to support and build host nation capacity in disbursing monies for immediate needs of salary, essential services, etc
	Establish simple and reliable capacity to process payments, and to record and report payments	Treasury USAID DOD			In hostile and uncertain environments, DOD should be prepared to support and build host nation capacity in establishing payment system
	Identify capacity to absorb and administer grants and foreign funds	Treasury USAID			An estimate of the country's absorptive capacity should be available from general economic assessment.
	Initiate simple and reliable system to manage grants and foreign assistance	Treasury USAID DOD			In hostile and uncertain environments, DOD should be prepared to support and build host nation capacity in receiving, accounting and administering donor grants

Category	Tasks	Agencies		Description
Budget	* Develop budget * Rationalize revenues and expenditures and establish priorities * Develop and implement a budgetary process, including input from line ministries	Treasury USAID DOC DOD		In hostile and uncertain environments, DOD should be prepared to support and build host nation capacity in budget preparation and execution, especially at the community level. In all environments and if civilian agencies are present to lead, DOD should participate and assist in prioritizing defense and security requirements. * DOC (BEA) can advise on national accounting standards
Public sector Investment	* Prioritize public investment needs* Develop a plan to allocate resources* Pay civil service arrears* Determine structure and affordable size of civil service to meet ongoing and future needs* Strengthen ethics regulations	State USAID DOD		In hostile and uncertain environments, DOD should be prepared to assist and build host nation capacity in identifying and prioritizing public investment needs, including organizational reform/improving civil service
	* Invest in critical projects neglected by the private sector (i.e., large-scale investment in education, health care, electricity, mining, oil, and public transportation)	USAID DOD		* In all environments, DOD should be prepared to assist and build host nation capacity in identifying the condition of critical infrastructure and essential services, and be prepared to repair/reconstruct critical elements. * Whole of government planning should identify any requirements for DOD providing special expertise, essential equipment (office equipment, computers, etc), physical rehabilitation, refurbish essential facilities, etc...
	* Select and train indigenous civil servants * Consider private-public investment partnerships			
Contracting and Procurement	* Establish transparent and reliable procurement system * Train line Ministries in procedures	USAID CLDP DOD		In all environments, DOD should be prepared to conduct transparent contracting; and support and build capacity in host nation to contract openly within a sound legal framework.

Category	Tasks	Agencies	Intl Org	Notes
Revenue Generation, Tax Administration	* Identify tax structure and sources of revenue * Design an efficient tax structure with a clear collection policy * Manage public accounts	Treasury USAID DOD	IMF World Bank	In hostile and uncertain environments, DOD should be prepared to assist and build host nation capacity in identifying tax sources, collecting taxes, fees, royalties, etc and managing those public accounts.
Border and Boundary Control (FROM SECURITY)	Establish border security, including customs regime to prevent arms smuggling, interdict contraband (i.e., drugs and natural resources), prevent trafficking of persons, regulate immigration and emigration, and establish control over major points of entry	DOD DHS Treasury DOC		
Customs Reform, Enforcement (See Trade, Trade Structure)	* Assess customs revenues and efficiencies and weaknesses of customs service* Identify immediate physical and capacity barriers to import administration* Take steps to open borders in a way that reduces incentives for corruption* Review and make recommendations on tariffs	Treasury USAID/DOC/DHS/DOD	World BankIntl Customs Org	In hostile and uncertain environments, DOD should be prepared to assist and build host nation capacity in evaluating customs operations and assist in border managementDOC has CLDP and NOAA capabilities* State can provide Export Control and Related Border Security (EXBS) assistance focused on developing and enhancing a country's capabilities to prevent proliferation and detect, interdict, and investigate illegal transfers of weapons and materials.
	* Ensure incentives in place to conduct efficient and non-corrupt customs service * Simplify the country's customs code for ease of administration for importers with low risk profile for evasion and smuggling * Assess magnitude of non-official international trade, and implications for revenues and economic activity particularly as it affects specific regions of the country or specific types of merchandise	Treasury USAID DOC DHS DOD	World Bank Intl Customs Org	* The DOC International Trade Administration, Market Access and Compliance, funds assessments of customs systems to understand the impact of customs corruption, the level of technical expertise on trade facilitation issues, and assess particular knowledge gaps so that the appropriate technical assistance can be deployed to improve trade between countries and the United States. * Technical assistance can be provided through USAID

	Tasks	Treasury USAID CLDP DHS DOD	World Bank Intl Customs Org
	* Undertake the training of customs personnel necessary to administer customs laws consistently nationwide * Establish laws and a legal structure that ensure accountability of the customs administration and the importing community * Expand port and border crossing capabilities with a view to administering higher volumes of trade	Treasury USAID CLDP DHS DOD	World Bank Intl Customs Org
Tax Policy	* Determine the efficacy of alternative short-term tax policies (i.e., tax holiday) * Identify and implement ST measures to increase revenue as appropriate - cognizant of effects on war torn population	Treasury USAIDD OD	
Fiscal Audit	* Identify audit capacity of relevant institution * Determine base line data for audit * Create or strengthen compliance laws		

FINANCIAL SUB-SECTOR

	Task	USG	IGO	NGO /Private Sector	Specify Agent(s) /Remarks
Banking Operations	* If banking sub-sector operational, start up commercial banking operations, i.e., open LOC mechanism and trade credits to reintegrate into the international financial community * If banking sub-sector operational, ensure capacity for bank payments and settlements * Evaluate conditions of banks and determine medium-term strategy for operations * Start-up or continue transparent and commercially viable bank operations * Review non-performing loan portfolio for bankrupt banks and decide how to address bank losses	USAID Treasury FRB DOD Support			Implementing commercial banking is civilian agency action, primarily US AID Treasury does not normally work with commercial banks
Banking Regulations and Oversight	* Evaluate the regulatory framework * Review and prepare bank licensing standards and procedures * Begin bank licensing process to ensure commercially viable private banks have access to the market * Set up supervisory and regulatory framework for banks * Prepare other prudential banking standards * Recruit and train regulators * Prepare manuals and standards for on-sight and off-sight bank inspections * Initiate inspections	Treasury FRB USAID			Assessment of regulatory framework and bank licensing procedures and priorities should be available from the general economic assessment Intermediate term civilian agency action

Category	Tasks				
	* Institutionalize regulatory system to govern financial transactions by banks* Monitor and Enforce banking regulations* Emphasize transparency in banking system to prevent corruption and enhance economic stability				
Bank Lending	* Provide immediate credit including access to micro and SME lending * Ensure standard banking practices to approve loans are part of early credit programs	USAID DOD	World Bank	CRS	In all environments, DOD should be prepared to request Contingency Contract Funding with the ability to provide micro-grants.
Asset and Money Laundering	* Establish Terrorist Financing Intelligence Unit * Freeze accounts of combatants * Block international access to overseas accounts, money laundering * Trace assets and remit back to the government	Treasury DOD	World Bank		Establish an Interagency Terrorist Finance Unit

DEBT

	Task	USG	IGO	NGO /Private Sector	Specify Agent(s) /Remarks
Arrears Clearance	* Conduct inventory of multilateral and bilateral arrears * Develop arrears clearance strategy (i.e., multilateral fund, debt forgiveness) * Make necessary payments to creditors	Treasury "Paris Club"		"London Club"	
Economic Enforcement and Anti-Corruption (See Fiscal Policy and Governance)	* Identify incentives to reduce corruption * Assess threat and existence of corruption in political system * Identify drivers of corruption * Develop laws promoting anti-corruption, accountability and transparency within government and private sector * Create mechanisms to curtail corruption, including special prosecutors, witness and judge protection, and ethics norms Assess threat/existence of corruption in political system	State USAID Treasury DOD	IMF World Bank UN		* Assessment should be available from general economic assessment completed in Appendix A. * Civilian agency led activity * DOD should use anti-corruption practices to deter corruption * Use public information to educate the public, report and fight corruption

Tasks	Agencies			Agencies
* Design and implement anti-corruption campaign, including education and codes of conduct * Enforce anti-corruption laws, including removal of corrupt officials * Develop and implement enforcement mechanisms * Combat corruption among police, border, customs, and tax collection forces/units	State USAID DOC DOD			* DOC CLDP
* Empower legal and civil society mechanisms to monitor governmental behavior* Foster transparent governing practices in public and private sectors* Revise procurement procedures				

Intentionally Blank

APPENDIX D
DEPARTMENT OF STATE ECONOMIC ENGAGEMENT MATRIX

Economic Indicators	Year	Units	Value
GDP per capita	2007	nominal $	
Nominal GDP	2007	$ mil.	
Global GDP Rank	2007	global	
Regional GDP Rank	2007	within region	
Real GDP	2007	2000$ mil.	
Real GDP Growth	2007	%	
Real GDP Avg. Growth	1997-2007	%	
Inflation	2007	%	
Avg. Inflation	1997-2007	%	
Population*	2007	thousand persons	

Engagement	Year	Units	Value
FTAs	as of 10/2008		
TIFAs	as of 10/2008		
Investment Treaties	as of 10/2008		
Air Service Agreements	as of 10/2008		
Other Agreements	as of 10/2008		
Investment Disputes	as of 10/2008	# - Profile	
GSP & Preferences	as of 10/2008		
GSP % Total Exports	2007	%	
Special 301	as of 10/2008		
WTO	as of 10/2008		
OECD	as of 10/2008		

Sub-sector Indicators	Year	Units	Value
Agriculture % GDP	2007	%	
Service % GDP	2007	%	
Industry % GDP	2007	%	
Exports % GDP	2007	%	
Imports % GDP	2007	%	

Development Aid	Year	Units	Value
US ODA	2006	$ mil.	
World ODA	2006	$ mil.	
US ODA % World ODA	2006	%	
Total Assistance Req	FY2009	$ mil.	
Econ Support Funds Req	FY2009	$ mil.	
TCB Activities	2007	$ thou.	
TDA Projects	2003-2007	$ thou [#]	

Trade and Investment	Year	Units	Value
Exports to US	2007	$ mil.	
Imports from US	2007	$ mil.	
Trade Balance w/US	2007	$ mil.	
US Trade (X+M)	2007	$ mil.	
World Trade (X+M)	2007	$ mil.	
US FDI Stock	2006	$ mil.	
Net FDI Inflows from US	2006	$ mil.	
Net FDI Inflows from World	2006	$ mil.	
Ex-Im Bank Exposure	FY2007	$ thou.	
OPIC Exposure	2007	$ mil.	

Development Indicators	Year	Units	Value
Anti-Corruption Agreement	As of 10/2008		
TI Corruption Index	2008	1=Corrupt, 10=Clean	
Heritage Econ Frdm	2008	Rank [Freedom %]	
Gini Income Inequality	1999-2004	0=Equal, 100=Unequal	
Population < $1/Day	1999-2004	% of pop.	
Doing Business Rank	2008	1=Best	
Adult Literacy	2007	% of pop.	
Womens Literacy	2007	% of pop.	
GTIP Rank	2007	Tier 1-3 (3 Worst)	
INCSR Drug Trafficking	2007		

Finance Indicators	Year	Units	Value
USG Debt Treatment	As of 10/2008	year	
USG Debt Forgiveness	As of 10/2008	$ mil.	
Current IMF Program	As of 10/2008		
FX Reserves	2007	$ mil.	
Money Laundering Status	As of 10/2008		
External Debt Stock	2007	$ mil.	
External Debt % GDP	2007	%	
Fiscal Balance % GDP	2007	%	
Market Cap	As of 10/2008	$ bil.	

Millennium Challenge	Year	Units	Value
(MCC) Status	2008	index (percentile)	
(MCC) Political Rights	2008	index (percentile)	
(MCC) Civil Liberties	2008	index (percentile)	
(MCC) Voice and Account.	2008	index (percentile)	
(MCC) Govt Effectiveness	2008	index (percentile)	

Millennium Challenge	Year	Units	Value
(MCC) Rule of Law	2008	index (percentile)	
(MCC) Control of Corruption	2008	index (percentile)	
(MCC) Girls Primary Compl.	2008	index (percentile)	
(MCC) Education Expend.	2008	index (percentile)	
(MCC) Health Expenditures	2008	index (percentile)	
(MCC) Immunization rate	2008	index (percentile)	
(MCC) Inflation	2008	index (percentile)	
(MCC) Fiscal Policy	2008	index (percentile)	
(MCC) Trade Policy	2008	index (percentile)	
(MCC) Regulatory Quality	2008	index (percentile)	
(MCC) Business Start Up	2008	index (percentile)	
(MCC) Land Rights Access	2008	index (percentile)	
(MCC) Ntrl Resource Mngmnt	2008	index (percentile)	

Telecommunications	Year	Units	Value
Telecom ITR	as of 10/2008	year	
WRC	as of 10/2008	year	
Cellular Penetration	2007	per 100 pop.	
Internet Penetration	2007	per 100 pop.	

Energy Indicators	Year	Units	Value
Oil Consumption	2006	thou. barrels / day	
Oil Production	2006	thou. barrels / day	
Energy Intensity	2005	BTU / rGDP 2000	
Energy Member	As of 10/2008	IEA/OPEC	

Government Finances	Year	Units	Value
Current Revenue	2006	% GDP	
Budget balance	2006	% GDP	
Overall Surplus/Deficit	2005	% GDP	

Employment	Year	Units	Value
Size of workforce	2007	Millions	
Employment by sub-sector	2007	List by %	
Unemployment	2007	%	
IDPs	2007	Millions	
Refugees	2007	Millions	
Ex-Combatants	2007	Millions	
In State Owned Enterprises	2007	Millions	

Defense Indicators	Year	Units	Value
Defense Spending		% GDP	
Defense Spending		% Budget	
Spending per capita/per member		$	
Arms Exports/Imports		Items/$	

Miscellaneous	Year	Units	Value
Remittances		% GDP	

Demographics	Year	Units	Value
Population	2007	thou. persons	
Ethnic Groups	2007	List by %	
Religions	2007	List by %	
Regional Distribution	2007	%	
Infant Mortality	2007	per 1,000	
Mortality rate	2007	per 1,000	
Literacy	2007	%	

Econ Infrastructure	Year	Units	Value
Electricity			
Water			
Rail & Road			
Airport & Seaport			

Natural Resources	Year	Units	Value

Geographic	Year	Units	Value

APPENDIX E
REFERENCES

1. Books and Articles

a. Albu, Mike and Alison Griffith, *Mapping the Market: A Framework for Rural Enterprise Policy and Practice*, Warwickshire, Practical Action, 2005.

b. Alex, Gary, Tom Remington and Philip Steffen. *Strengthening Agricultural Markets in Areas Affected by Conflict*, Agricultural Investment Note for the Agricultural Investment Sourcebook, The World Bank, Washington, D.C., 2006. Further information about this publication can be found at the World Bank agriculture and rural development website http://web.worldbank.org/.

c. Beasely, Kenneth W. 2006. *Job creation in post conflict Societies*, PPC issues paper No. 9, PN-ADE-194, USAID.

d. Binnendijk, Hans and Stuart E. Johnson, *Transforming for Stabilization and Reconstruction Operations*, Center for Technology and National Security Policy, National Defense University Press, Washington, DC, 2004.

e. Cook, Nicolas, *Liberia: Transition to Peace,* CRS Report to Congress, Congressional Research Service, Washington, DC, updated October 24, 20.

2. Joint and Service Publications

a. US Army FM 3-07. *Stability Operations*, 5 September 2008.

b. JP 3-07, *Stability Operations* (First Draft), 25 November 2009.

c. JP 3-08, *Interorganizational Coordination During Joint Operations* (Revision First Draft), 28 August 2009.

d. JP 3-57, *Civil-Military Operations*, 8 July 2008.

e. JP 4-10, *Operational Contract Support*, 17 October 2008.

f. JP 5-0, *Joint Operation Planning*, 26 December 2006.

3. Agency and Organization Issuances

a. Development in Stabilization and Reconstruction Operations International Labor Organization, *Poverty and Employment in Crisis Situation: The gender dimension*, May 2003.

b. Dutch Committee for Afghanistan–Veterinary Programmes (DCA-VET). *Continuation of the Afghan Veterinary Privatization Effort to Secure Sustainability of the Veterinary Field Unit (VFU) System established under USAID-RAMP.* http://www.dca-vet nl/DCA/documents 07JansummarysheetASAPproject_000.pdf.

c. Joint Center for Operational Analysis, U.S. Joint Forces Command, *Provincial Reconstruction Teams in Afghanistan – An Interagency Assessment,* 2006.

d. Longley, Catherine, Ian Christoplos and Tom Slaymaker. *Agricultural Rehabilitation: Mapping the linkages between humanitarian relief, social protection, and development.* Humanitarian Policy Group Research Report 22. London: Overseas Development Institute, April 2006.

e. Miehlbradt, Alexandra O. and Mary McVay. *Implementing Private sector Development: Striving for Tangible Results for the Poor,* The 2006 Reader.

f. Miller, Dan and Dave Sherman. *Privatization of Veterinary Services: Development that Works.* USAID/Afghanistan, January 2006.

g. Nourse, Tim, Tracy Gerstle, Alex Snelgrove, David Rinck and Mary McVay. SEEP Market Development Working Group. *Market Development in Crisis-Affected Environments: Emerging Lessons for Achieving Pro-Poor Economic Reconstruction,* Washington, DC, 2007.

h. Sperling, Louise and Tom Remington with Jon M. Haugen, *Seed Aid for Seed Security: Advice for Practitioners,* Rome: International Center for Tropical Agriculture and Catholic Relief Services. http://www.crs.org/publications/agriculture.cfm, 2006.

i. Tarnoff, Curt, *Iraq: Reconstruction Assistance,* CRS Report to Congress, Congressional Research Service, Washington, D.C., updated May 22, 2008.

j. United Nations, Development Program Commission on the Private sector and Development, *Unleashing Entrepreneurship: Making Business Work for the Poor,* 2004.

k. US Agency for International Development, *Bosnia and Herzegovina Strategic Plan Summary,* Washington, D.C., updated August 23, 2006.

l. USAID, Bureau for Economic Growth, Agriculture, and Trade, Economic Growth Office, *A Guide to Economic Growth in Post-Conflict Countries (draft),* Oct 4, 2007.

m. USAID, *Community Based Development in Conflict Areas – an Introductory Guide for Programming,* 2007.

n. USAID, Office of Conflict Management and Mitigation, *Conducting a Conflict Assessment: A Framework for Strategy and Program Development,* 2004.

o. USAID/Conflict Management and Mitigation, *Land and Conflict: A Toolkit for Programming,* 2004.

p. USAID, *Livelihoods and conflict – A Toolkit for Intervention,* 2005.

q. US Department of State. April, 2005. *Post-Conflict Reconstruction Essential Tasks*. US Department of State, Office of the Coordinator for Reconstruction and Stabilization.

r. US Institute for Peace, *Employment Generation and Economic Development in Stabilization and Reconstruction Operations*, March 2007.

s. Vonnegut, Andrew and Kimberly Kotnik. November 2006. *Using Markets in Conflict Mitigation: Conceptual and Practical Considerations*. Belgrade: Booz Allen Hamilton.

t. World Bank, *Doing Business*, 2008.

u. World Bank, *Managing Agricultural Risk, Vulnerability, and Disaster*, Agriculture Investment Sourcebook, Module 11. Further information about this publication can be found at the World Bank agriculture and rural development website http://web.worldbank.org/.

Intentionally Blank

APPENDIX F
ENDNOTES

[1] US Agency for International Development. A Guide to Economic Growth in Post-Conflict Countries, pg. vi (2009).

[2] ibid.

[3] Kathleen H. Hicks et al, "The Future of US Civil Affairs Forces", Center for Strategic & International Studies, Washington DC, February 2009, pg. 44.

[4] JP 1-02, *Department of Defense Dictionary of Military and Associated Terms*, 48.

[5] *M&E Fundamentals: A Self-Guided Minicourse*, USAID, Jan 07, 3.

[6] Ibid, 5.

[7] In current operations overseas, the Commander's Emergency Response Program (CERP) utilizes CCO-appointed representatives better known as Project Purchasing Officers or PPOs.

[8] OECD Principles for Good International Engagement in Fragile States, 20 March 2007.

[9] ibid.

[10] US Institute for Peace, *The Quest for Viable Peace*, USIP Press, 2005 and OSD *Measuring Progress in a Conflict Environment*, August 2008.

[11] March 2007 Interagency Management System.

[12] www.state.gov.

[13] http://www.imf.org.

[14] http://www.web.worldbank.org.

[15] http://www reliefweb.int.

[16] http://www.undp.org.

[17] http://www.wto.org.

[18] http://www.icao.int

[19] www.oecd.org/dac.

[20] Hostile environment: An operational environment in which hostile forces have control as well as intent and capability to effectively oppose or adversely react to the operations a unit intends to conduct. JP 3-0.

[21] Uncertain environment: An operational environment in which host government forces do not have effective control of the territory and population in the intended operational area, whether opposed to or receptive to operations that a unit intends to conduct. JP 3-0.

[22] "Losing the Golden Hour" James Stephenson, page 36.

[23] Beasely, Kenneth W. 2006. Job creation in post conflict Societies, PPC issues paper No. 9, PN-ADE-194, USAID.

[24] The United Nations High Commissioner for Refugees (UNHCR) Quick Impact Projects (QiPs: A Provisional Guide.

[25] USAID-IG Audit E-267-08-001-P, "Audit of USAID/Iraq's Community Stabilization Program," March 18, 2008.

[26] Special Economic Zones, Performance, Lessons Learned and Implications for Zone Development, FIAS World Bank Group, April 2008.

[27] USIP Special Report, Employment Generation and Economic Development in Stabilization and Reconstruction Operation.

[28] See United Nations Integrated DDR Standards (IDDRS), also Secretary-General, note to the General Assembly, A/C.5/59/31, New York, NY, May 2005.

[29] USIP Special Report, Employment Generation and Economic Development in Stabilization and Reconstruction Operation.

[30] World Bank Development Report 2005.

[31] http://go.worldbank.org/6IQR415UN0.

[32] http://www.doingbusiness.org/.

[33] http://www.microlinks.org.

[34] http://www.cgap.org.

[35] *Contingency Contracting: A Joint Handbook for the 21st Century.* http://www.acq.osd mil/dpap/pacc/cc/jcchb/.

[36] US Department of State, *Interagency Management System for Reconstruction & Stabilization*, 9 March 2007, page 2.

[37] US Army, FM 3-07, Stability Operations, October 2008, page 2-5.

[38] The Tactical Conflict Assessment Framework is a standardized diagnostic process designed for use by both military and civilian personnel. It is employed to gather information from local inhabitants to identify the causes of instability or conflict in tactical areas of operation. This

information helps identify, prioritize, monitor, evaluate, and adjust civil-military programming targeted at diminishing the causes of instability or conflict.

[39] http://www.fas.usda.gov/excredits/foodaid/ffe/mcdfactsheet.asp.

[40] http://www.fao.org.

[41] http://www.ers.usda.gov.

[42] http://www.nsa.smil mil/producer/refs/eiu.

[43] Economic Impact of Peacekeeping; Michael Carnahan, William Durch, Scott Gilmore March 2006.

[44] See Financial Management Regulation (FMR), Volume 12, Chapter 27, Section 270204, paragraph G.

[45] "Gender-relevant policy performance" refers to the performance of policies designed specifically to aid women. Such policies are often employed to redress historical disadvantages or imbalances, or to compensate for social tendencies deemed counter-productive to economic advancement.

[46] https://www.intelink.gov/diplopedia/matrix.

[47] http://www.nsa.smil mil/producer/refs/eiu.

[48] http://go.worldbank.org/JD8TRDFQ60 and http://go.worldbank.org/8QTPOHBME0.

[49] http://lcweb2.loc.gov/frd/cs/cshome.html.

[50] http://go.worldbank.org/1SF48T40L0.

[51] http://go.worldbank.org/XA79EUBIQ0 and http://go.worldbank.org/8QTPOHBME0.

[52] www.unhcr.org/statistics/populationdatabase.

[53] http://go.worldbank.org/QGUCPJTOR0 and http://www.ifad.org/events/remittances/maps/index htm.

[54] http://www.imf.org.

[55] www. OECD.org under Aid Statistics.

[56] http://www.intelink.sgov.gov/Reference/Janes.

[57] http://go.worldbank.org/JD8TRDFQ60.

[58] http://sedac.ciesin.columbia.edu/gpw/index.jsp.

59 http://www.who.int/whosis/whostat/en/.

60 http://go.worldbank.org/DCACK3M3F1 and http://www.census.gov/ipc/www/idb/index.php.

61 http://www.weforum.org/en/initiatives/gcp/index htm.

62 The reports are accessible through the IMF Web site, http://www.imf.org under the Country Info tab.

63 All are available at http://inrweb.state.sgov.gov/IA.html.

64 Principles of Interagency Conflict Assessment Framework.

65 US Agency for International Development. A Guide to Economic Growth in Post-Conflict Countries, (2007).

66 USAID Conflict Assessment Framework, at http://www.usaid.gov/our_work/cross-cutting_programs/conflict/publications/conflict_assessments html.

67 USACE Measuring Progress in Conflict Environments Version 1.0 August 1, 2008.

GLOSSARY
PART I—ABBREVIATIONS AND ACRONYMS

ASEAN	Association of Southeast Asian Nations
CAPT	civil affairs planning team
CCO	contingency contracting officer
CERP	Commander's Emergency Response Program
CIPE	Center for International Private Enterprise
COCO	chief of contracting office
COM	chief of mission
CMOC	civil military operations center
CRSG	country reconstruction and stabilization group
CSP	community stabilization program
DART	disaster assistance response team
DDR	disarmament, demobilization, and reintegration
DIME	diplomatic, informational, military, and economic
DNA	Diaspora Networks Alliance
DOC	Department of Commerce
DOD	Department of Defense
DODI	Department of Defense Instruction
DOL	Department of Labor
EIU	Economic Intelligence Unit
ERS	Economic Research Service
EX-IM	Export Import Bank
FAO	Food and Agriculture Organization
FAS	Foreign Agriculture Service
FIAS	Foreign Investment Advisory Service
FSO	foreign service officer
HA/DR	humanitarian assistance/ disaster relief
HHS	Department of Health and Human Services
HN	host nation
ICAF	interagency conflict assessment framework
ICAO	International Civil Aviation Organization
IDP	Internally Displaced Person
ILO	International Labor Organization
IMS	Interagency Management System
IPC	Interagency Policy Committee
ITA	International Trade Administration
JCMOTF	joint civil military operations task force
JFC	joint force commander

JOA	joint operational area
JOPP	joint operational planning process
JP	joint publication
JS	joint staff
JTF	joint task force
LOO	line of operations
M&E	monitoring and evaluation
MME	major mission element
NGO	nongovernmental organization
NOAA	National Oceanography and Atmospheric Agency
NSC	National Security Council
OECD	Organization for Economic Cooperation and Development
OFDA	Office of Foreign Disaster Assistance
OPIC	Overseas Private Investment Corporation
OSD	Office of the Secretary of Defense
OTI	Office of Transition Initiatives
PMESII	political, military, economic, social, infrastructure, and information
PRT	provincial reconstruction team
SCO	senior contracting official
S/CRS	Department of State Coordinator for Reconstruction and Stabilization
SEZ	special economic zone
SME	subject matter expert
SOE	state owned enterprise
SSR	security sector reform
SWEAT	sewer, water, electricity, academics, and trash
UN	United Nations
UNDP	United Nations Development Program
UNHCR	United Nations High Commissioner for Refugees
UNOCHA	United Nations Office for the Coordination of Humanitarian Affairs
US	United States
USAID	United States Agency for International Development
USDA	Department of Agriculture
USG	United States Government
USTDA	United States Trade and Development Agency
WFP	World Food Program
WTO	World Trade Organization

PART II—TERMS AND DEFINITIONS

area of responsibility. The geographical area associated with a combatant command within which a geographic combatant commander has authority to plan and conduct operations. Also called **AOR**. (JP 3-0)

civil affairs. Designated Active and Reserve component forces and units organized, trained, and equipped specifically to conduct civil affairs activities and to support civil-military operations. Also called **CA**. (JP 3-57)

combatant command. A unified or specified command with a broad continuing mission under a single commander established and so designated by the President, through the Secretary of Defense and with the advice and assistance of the Chairman of the Joint Chiefs of Staff. Combatant commands typically have geographic or functional responsibilities. (JP 5-0)

communication strategy. A joint force commander's strategy for coordinating and synchronizing themes, messages, images, and actions to support SC-related objectives and ensure the integrity and consistency of themes and messages to the lowest tactical level. (JP 3-0 RFD)

defense support to public diplomacy. Those activities and measures taken by the Department of Defense components to support and facilitate public diplomacy efforts of the United States Government. Also called **DSPD**. (JP 3-13)

drivers of conflict. An internal or external source of instability pushing parties within an R&S environment towards open conflict. (USG Planning Framework for Reconstruction, Stabilization, and Conflict Transformation)

end state. The set of required conditions that defines achievement of the commander's objectives. (JP 3-0)

economic stabilization. The process by which economic drivers of conflict and instability are managed and reduced, while efforts are made to support preconditions for successful longer-term economic growth in order to establish a stable and predictable economic environment.

fiscal policy. Revenue and expenditure structures as well as management techniques that allow a government to manage the economy through the expansion and contraction of government spending. (See Department of State Supplemental Reference: Foreign Assistance Standardized Program Structure and Definitions, Program Element 4.1.1, 12/12/2008)

humanitarian assistance. Programs conducted to relieve or reduce the results of natural or manmade disasters or other endemic conditions such as human pain, disease, hunger, or privation that might present a serious threat to life or that can result in great damage to or loss of property. Humanitarian assistance provided by US forces is limited in scope and duration. The assistance provided is designed to supplement or complement the efforts of the host nation civil authorities or agencies that may have the primary responsibility for providing humanitarian assistance. Also called HA. (JP 3-57)

information operations. The integrated employment of the core capabilities of electronic warfare, computer network operations, psychological operations, military deception, and operations security, in concert with specified supporting and related capabilities, to influence, disrupt, corrupt or usurp adversarial human and automated decision making while protecting our own. Also called **IO**. (JP 3-13)

instruments of national power. All of the means available to the government in its pursuit of national objectives. They are expressed as diplomatic, economic, informational and military. (JP 1)

interagency. United States Government agencies and departments, including the Department of Defense. See also interagency coordination. (JP 3-08)

interagency management system. An institutionalized system of interagency bodies (Country Reconstruction and Stabilization Group (CRSG), Integration Planning Cell (IPC), Advance Civilian Team (ACT), and Field Advance Civilian Team (FACT)) that manage the whole-of-government stabilization and reconstruction planning and operations. (USG Planning Framework for Reconstruction, Stabilization, and Conflict Transformation)

intergovernmental organization. An organization created by a formal agreement (e.g., a treaty) between two or more governments. It may be established on a global, regional, or functional basis for wide-ranging or narrowly defined purposes. Formed to protect and promote national interests shared by member states. Examples include the United Nations, North Atlantic Treaty Organization, and the African Union. Also called **IGO**. (JP 3-08)

joint force. A general term applied to a force composed of significant elements, assigned or attached, of two or more Military Departments operating under a single joint force commander. (JP 3-0)

joint task force. A joint force that is constituted and so designated by the Secretary of Defense, a combatant commander, a subunified commander, or an existing joint task force commander. Also called **JTF**. (JP 1)

major mission element. The elements of the plan that are necessary and sufficient to achieve the overarching policy goal. MMEs should be cross-sectoral, stated as outcomes, and based on an analysis of the conflict. (USG Planning Framework for Reconstruction, Stabilization, and Conflict Transformation)

message. A narrowly focused communication directed at a specific audience to create a specific effect while supporting a theme. (JP 1-02)

monetary policy. Monetary policy refers to the actions undertaken by a central bank to influence the availability and cost of money and credit as a means of helping to promote national economic goals. (US Federal Reserve)

narrative. Enduring strategic communication with context, reason/motive, and goal/end state. (JP 1-02)

nongovernmental organization. A private, self-governing, not-for-profit organization dedicated to alleviating human suffering; and/or promoting education, health care, economic development, environmental protection, human rights, and conflict resolution; and/or encouraging the establishment of democratic institutions and civil society. Also called **NGO**. (JP 3-08)

operational environment. A composite of the conditions, circumstances, and influences that affect the employment of capabilities and bear on the decisions of the commander. (JP 3-0)

public affairs. Those public information, command information, and community relations activities directed toward both the external and internal publics with interest in the Department of Defense. Also called **PA**. See also **command information; community relations; public information**. (JP 3-61)

rule of law. The rule of law refers to a principle of governance in which all persons, institutions and entities, public and private, including the State itself, are accountable to laws that are publicly promulgated, equally enforced, and independently adjudicated, and which are consistent with international human rights norms and standards. It requires, as well, measures to ensure adherence to the principles of supremacy of law, equality before the law, accountability to the law, fairness in the application of the law, separation of powers, participation in decision-making, legal certainty, avoidance of arbitrariness, and procedural and legal transparency. (USAID, Department of Defense, and Department of State Guidance on Security Sector Reform at 4, Jan 15, 2009. See also UN Doc. S/2004/616 (2004), para.6. See also UN Doc. A/61/636-S/2006/980 (2006).)

stability operations. An overarching term encompassing various military missions, tasks, and activities conducted outside the United States in coordination with other instruments of national power to maintain or reestablish a safe and secure environment, provide essential governmental services, emergency infrastructure reconstruction, and humanitarian relief. (JP 3-0)

Intentionally Blank

Military Support To Economic Stabilization

www.ingramcontent.com/pod-product-compliance
Lightning Source LLC
Chambersburg PA
CBHW081326310526
45789CB00018B/2443

* 9 7 8 1 5 0 0 5 0 8 8 0 7 *